READING HENRY JAMES

READING
HENRY JAMES

by Louis Auchincloss

UNIVERSITY OF MINNESOTA
PRESS, MINNEAPOLIS

For Leon Edel
Friend and Mentor

The caricatures of Henry James by Max Beerbohm are reproduced by the permission of Mrs. Eva Reichmann. All but one are catalogued in *A Catalogue of the Caricatures of Max Beerbohm*, compiled by Rupert Hart-Davis. Earlier versions of the chapters "Henry James: The Man and Artist," "The Virtuous Attachment: *The Ambassadors*," and "James's Literary Use of His American Tour" appeared in *Show, Horizon*, and the *South Atlantic Quarterly*.

Contents

Illustrations

READING HENRY JAMES

Henry James:
The Man and Artist

Henry James did not abandon his country, as he is often accused of doing; he never really took it up. It was not his fault that as a child he had to live abroad for years at a time, in London, Paris, Geneva, Bonn, constantly changing his schools and languages. The lives of the James children were determined by a whimsical, utterly charming, maddeningly open-minded father, the Swedenborgian philosopher, who varied his domiciles to accord with his theories of education and to fit with the fluctuations of an inherited income. Even in America, Henry James, Sr., could not settle on an abode; he moved his family from Albany to New York to Newport to Boston and finally to Cambridge. There was no place, except perhaps briefly Newport, that young Henry ever considered home.

A very simple fact is that mid-Victorian London and Second Empire Paris were bound to make a greater impression on a sensitive small boy than their contemporary New York or Boston. The future novelist very sensibly adapted himself to the circumstances of his wandering life and became an ardent sightseer. He later claimed that his first memory, dating from his second year, was a glimpse of the column of the Place Vendôme framed by the window of the carriage in which he was riding. And as sightseers are apt to be concerned with the past as revealed in the more picturesque aspects of its decay, so was James all his life to see the past in the light of romance and the present in the light of something less. There was always to be a guidebook side in his approach to sites and cities, and the thrill of the boy peering over the bow of the big white Cunarder for a first glimpse of "Europe" was to be as fresh for him at seventy as at seven.

From the picturesque and the romantic it was an easy step to the glorious. Leon Edel points out that the objects which appealed to the young Henry's imagination in the Louvre were all of this nature. "The note of glory is struck repeatedly: glory on the heroic, Napoleonic scale. The very paintings he mentions are of people in high places, the assassinated and beheaded, whose glory was ephemeral as well: the Princes in the Tower, Charles I, Lady Jane Grey." "Style" was associated in James's young mind with the Louvre, the Luxembourg, empire, royalty. Years later, in reading of the celebrations of the Prince Imperial's baptism in *Eugène Rougon*, he wondered if the young Zola had been that day a dazzled boy in the same shouting crowds with him.

But what had all this glory — martial glory, at that — to do with a tense, feverishly imaginative lad, of unrobust health, who did not join his contemporaries in any of the sports or activities that developed masculine prowess, and whose wandering, unconventional father was not even in "business," let alone politics or the army? How was he to attain it? There seems never to have been even a moment when he contemplated reaching his goal through a life of action, and his studies in engineering and law were purely to oblige the eccentric Swedenborgian. In his own mind, art was always his only road to glory, as the Church in the Middle Ages had been that for those not born for military combat. The only effective way to deal with a world that was stronger, better organized, and essentially *different* from oneself was to turn it into artistic source material.

If he had not been sure of this before the Civil War, that catastrophe would have convinced him. Because of an "obscure hurt," probably to his back, he was unable to serve in the army and spent those first years of carnage with the women in Newport, the Newport of pre-tycoon days, which he was ever after to describe in such terms as "shy," "sweet," and "modest," contrasting it, consciously or not, with the raging horror of the battlefields from which he had been absent. One cannot but wonder if the "hurt," which did not prevent him, apparently, from leading a normal life, was really sufficient, at least in the depths of his own conscience, to exempt him from service. It does not stretch the imagination to see him committed thereafter to a life without sex because he had failed as a man, by his own inner lights, at a time when it counted most to be one. He was a celibate now, a "churchman" by necessity as well as by choice.

When the young men returned after Appomattox, the bronzed, hardened young men, like his friend Oliver Wendell Holmes, Jr., still in uniform, to receive all the attention of the female cousins and friends, when America turned its energies to the making of money instead of the shedding of blood, relegating literature and Henry James to the "uptown" parlors of dancing masters and teas, how could he do better than to escape again to Europe and go "reeling and moaning" through the streets of a newly discovered Rome in a fever of aesthetic enjoyment? Is it even surprising that he should have defended himself against American tourists by shrilly describing them to his brother William as "vulgar, vulgar, vulgar"?

Certainly, the young and rapidly middle-aging man, very grave, but with the look of an Elizabethan sea captain, who settled at last in London, was as totally dedicated an artist as ever existed. To see, to observe, *that* was to live. The damp, dark, dusky, magnificent hulk of the British capital was crammed with all the life he could use, from the remnants of a Georgian aristocracy with its white-winged coachmen to the teeming slums that he would copy for *The Princess Casamassima*. We hear that he dined out one hundred and forty times in one winter and catch this glimpse of him: "A rather dark and decidedly handsome young man of medium height, with a full beard, stood in the doorway and bowed rather stiffly, as if he were not to be confused with the rank and file of his compatriots." A compelling reason for living abroad was precisely that one was not classed, not ranked. One could stand aside, in perfect detachment, observe, record, and create. When Minny Temple, the beautiful young cousin across the water, died of consumption, he might have lamented her as a friend, even bemoaned her as an imagined love, but he had gained her as a subject. He was never really to lose anyone again.

From the start he supported himself. Even after he had inherited his bit of the diminished family capital, he turned the income over to his sister. No writer was ever more professional. The bulk of James's work exceeds that of any other American writer of note. In this first period, he produced book reviews, drama and art criticism, newspaper columns, travel pieces and travel books, short stories, novelettes, a biography, and two novels — *Roderick Hudson* and *The American*. His fiction had many themes, including the romantic and even the melodramatic, but one predominated, with which his name was ever after to be associated, the "international theme" of the effect of Americans and Europeans on each other, the former usually cast as heroes or heroines, the parvenu millionaire or the debutante from Schenectady, having in common a certain high boldness, innocence, and ingenuousness, and the latter in the roles of villains, even murderers, corrupted by an older, richer, darker culture. James might seem to sympathize with the innocent victims, but he had thrown in his lot with their undoers. It was a triumph over the "shy, sweet, modest" Newport of his youth, but the heroine of "Daisy Miller," his sole "best seller," was to win the last round, for it was always to irritate him that his name became synonymous with hers.

Daisy Millers were all very well, but he was after bigger things. Speaking of his future as a writer, he had confided to his brother his hopes of becoming a "sufficiently great man." He conceived of his assault on the literary world in terms of a conquest, and Napoleon, as shown by the special red morocco in which the copies of the marshals' memoirs were rebound for his library, was always the towering figure of his imagination. The only figure in literary history who might be mentioned in the same breath with Napoleon was Balzac, and Balzac became his model. The French novelist had set his titanic energies to no less a task than to re-create France, and James turned now to the creation of his own *comédie humaine*. Yes, if one was not to be a soldier or a statesman, or even a businessman or a father, one might still be the peer of all by becoming a Balzac.

He gave up the intense social life of his earlier years. He continued to see his friends and to travel, but more as a diversion than in the quest of material. That, at forty, he basically had — a sackful of impressions that would last a lifetime, though situations, *données*, as he called them, were always to be suggested in the chatter of acquaintances and carefully recorded in his notebooks. In a few driving years, he now produced a body of work that would have assured his ultimate reputation had he died at forty-seven. Yet few indeed were the readers in 1890 who would have known it.

It is difficult to see why the great novels of this middle or "Balzac" period did not do better with the public. There was no other writer of the eighties — certainly in America — who could approach James in the dazzling virtuosity of his style or in the vitality of his characterizations, and one would have thought there were subjects for every taste. *The Bostonians*, American to the core, satirizes the movement for women's emancipation in a cause-mad, meeting-mad, charity-mad New England, and its atmosphere is tense with the antagonism between the sexes; *The Tragic Muse*, thoroughly English, dramatizes the ancient conflict, in two young aristocrats, between the arts and the conventional professions; *The Princess Casamassima* explores the world of poverty and plotted revolution in the slums of London. And in *The Portrait of a Lady*, the masterpiece of the period, James wrote a determinist novel in the tradition of Flaubert about an idealistic American girl doomed by her own impetuous generosity to become the victim, not this time of a corrupted Europe, but, by a clever twist, of two other Americans already so

"A Nightmare. Mr Henry James subpoena'd, as psychological expert, in a *cause célèbre*." The legend Max Beerbohm provided for his 1908 caricature reads: "Cross-examining Counsel: 'Come, sir, I ask you a plain question, and I expect a plain answer!'"

corrupted. But whatever the reason, he did not sell — at least as he had hoped.

It was now that he made his first major foray into the great world of intenser competition that he had always eschewed. It was to be a strictly limited one, so as to take as little time as possible from his "poor blest old Genius," but it was at the same time to supply this Genius with adequate revenues. The theater would be the answer to everything, and he exulted at how neatly that key promised to fit his lock. Had he not always loved the drama? Did he not have the French playwrights "in his pocket"? It is almost incredible that he should have thought so. One can only gape at the temerity of the man who could consider that such hollow, chattering, contrived, and heartless parlor comedies as *Disengaged* and *Tenants* were rivals of the work of Augier, Pailleron, or even Dumas *fils*. Everything about the abortive theater years, from his jubilant reporting of provincial first nights to his sending his servants to supply the rehearsing casts with sandwiches, strikes a euphoric note. Only when he stood before the footlights after the disastrous first night of *Guy Domville* and received full in the face the hisses and boos of the London crowd did he recognize the old hard Philistine world that he had tried to delude himself into thinking a friend. There would be no repetition of such errors.

In his notebook he recorded his rededication to his muse in solemn and moving lines. As Racine, after the triumph of *Phèdre*, gave up the theater for God, so did James, after the failure of all his plays, give it up for the god of fiction. But his deity was to reward his sacrifice.

Within three years, 1902 to 1904, as he approached and passed sixty, in rapid succession appeared his three greatest novels: *The Wings of the Dove, The Ambassadors*, and *The Golden Bowl. The Ambassadors* is the perfect finale to four decades of cogitation on the international problem. Gone is the idea of the corruption of an ingenuous and innocent America by an ancient, oversophisticated culture. Daisy Miller and Isabel Archer are relegated to the past; their creator had seen America rise to a position where its gold could corrupt Europe. Chad Newsome in Paris is lightly entangled with a woman whom he will abandon — that is as dangerous as poor old Paris has become. But American ingenuousness is enshrined and preserved in the person of Lambert Strether, a middle-aged widower, the editor of a New England literary quarterly, a kindly William Dean Howells (on whom indeed he was in part modeled) who has been to Europe once before, and then briefly, and now comes to rescue the erring Chad. There is no question, except humorously, of Strether's being corrupted. On the contrary, he is redeemed, renewed, stretched, by the Old World. The essence of the novel is the impression that Paris makes on Strether's mind, and hence on ours, the effect on an unspoiled, unsophisticated intelligence of the great bright shimmering city saturated with its splendid and heroic past. Strether in the end has failed in his mission and alienated his patroness; he will return to Woollett, as he tells Miss Gostrey, with the sole logic of having gained nothing for himself. But we know that he has gained his vision and that his vision will sustain him.

The elaborate style of the later novels has been the subject of unending jokes. Everyone knows that the James of these years was called the "old pretender" and likened to a hippopotamus in search of a pea. And his characters reminded E. M. Forster of "the exquisite deformities who haunted Egyptian art in the reign of Akhenaton — huge heads and tiny legs." Even such a friend and admirer as Edith Wharton accused James of stripping his people of all the fringes that human beings necessarily trail after them through life and suspending them in a Crookes tube.

All of this criticism might have had more validity had James, like most modern writers, been concerned with consciousness, with physical awareness, but he was not. He .was concerned with intelligence and sensibility; he was trying to create the drama of the perfect intelligence, the finest sensibility when confronted — which is simply the drama of civilization — with lesser intelligences and cruder sensibilities. A great deal has been written about "evil" in the later novels, and this may be an appropriate

term to describe the force with which their protagonists
are confronted, but it was not, at least to the author's private mind, a very dire evil. He would never, for example,
have denounced Kate Croy, in *The Wings of the Dove*, or
Charlotte Stant, in *The Golden Bowl*, as he was in 1914, at a
lunch party given by a pro-German American friend, hys-
terically to denounce the Kaiser. Kate wants her fiancé to
marry the dying heiress who loves him in order to inherit a
fortune, but she considers it a brilliant, even a beneficent,
stratagem from which all three will benefit. Charlotte
commits adultery with her husband's son-in-law, but she
believes, with much apparent justification, that her husband and stepdaughter are too preoccupied with each
other to notice or even much to care. The evil in Kate and
Charlotte is simply what is *not* in their natures and what *is*
in Milly's and Maggie's — a magnanimous, bottomless love
and sincerity.

Since this "evil" is defined in negatives, there is no advantage to seeing it in terms of physically ugly things. In
setting the backgrounds of these last novels — the great
soft luminous English country house in a drowsy summer-
time, the gleaming, glinting Adam Verver collection of
European masterpieces, the golden grace of the high
rooms in a Venetian palazzo — James was intentionally
fitting the richest kind of integument around his prime
intelligences; he was gilding the frame in which most fit-
tingly to present their moral beauty. It is true that we have
no homely glimpses — there are no bathrooms, no laun-
dries, no sculleries — but the readers who want such do
not realize (or do not care) that they would pay for them
with the effect of the whole.

James in his earlier days had distinctly failed to appreciate the French impressionist painters. He had a lean-

The master faces his younger self in this 1906
caricature of James by Beerbohm

ing for the detailed, brightly colorful, precisely represen-
tational canvases of the academic school that had at least
seemed, in his middle period, to be trying to do in the
visual arts what he had been trying to do in fiction. But he
came in time to revise his judgment and to become himself
the master impressionist of the novel. In his last works he
abandoned, almost totally, exact description and substi-
tuted a long series of dazzling metaphors. Prince Amerigo
in *The Golden Bowl* is seen largely in his association with

palace portraits, with objects of art, with fine old dark, even sinister things. We learn that his eyes are dark blue, but this is little to our knowledge that they resemble "the high windows of a Roman palace, of an historic front by one of the great old designers, thrown open on a feast-day to the golden air." And the Venice whose rainy weather changes to autumn sunshine just as the doomed Milly's illness enters its final phase irradiates later chapters of *The Wings of the Dove*: "Venice glowed and plashed and called and chimed again; the air was like a clap of hands, and the scattered pinks, yellows, blues, sea-greens, were like a hanging-out of vivid stuffs, a laying down of fine carpets."

From the publication of *The Golden Bowl* in 1904 to his death twelve years later in the war that induced him, after four decades of British residence, to become a British subject, James produced no more novels, though he left two unfinished ones. The last years were devoted largely to putting his house in order, to reminiscence and autobiography, and to the great and much (though, in my opinion, wrongly) deplored task of revising a lifetime's fiction for the twenty-four-volume Scribner edition. They were also the years of apotheosis, the years when the "master," in his brick Georgian ivy-covered house at Rye, was cultivated by the cognoscenti with a devotion that went far to make up for the neglect of the masses.

How he would have loved his posthumous fame! One can imagine Emily Brontë and Herman Melville shrugging shoulders, faintly scornful, but James would have bristled with pride at every mention of his name in every college catalogue. It is pleasant to think that in the end he had at least a whiff of it and that the silent, grave, bearded young man should have evolved into the portly figure of the rolling, resolute gait, simple in emotion but quick and spontaneous in affection, leaving among his recording disciples a deep impression of majesty, beauty, and greatness. The man who had merged his identity with that of the artist reemerged a finer man from the process. Here is A. C. Benson's last glimpse of him, just before his death: "He was lunching at the Athenaeum, and I went up to him — he had a companion — and said that I only came for a passing benediction. He put his hand on my arm and said: 'My dear Arthur, my mind is so constantly and continuously bent upon you in wonder and good will that any change in my attitude could be only the withholding of a perpetual and settled felicitation.' He uttered his little determined, triumphant laugh, and I saw him no more."

The Notebooks

Henry James's notebooks, edited by F. O. Matthiessen and Kenneth B. Murdock and first published in 1947, constitute the most illuminating records that we have of the creative process at work in the mind of a master novelist. The entries run from 1878 to 1911. As the editors put it: "Ideas for stories appear sometimes merely as bare statements, but more often with comments on the possibilities James saw in them. Often, too, there are further entries working out the technical problems presented, and showing how the finished story or novel took shape."

Many readers in 1947 were shocked by the seeming triviality of the themes which appealed to James. From the first to the last of more than three decades of entries there is hardly one that deals with the plight of the underprivileged, the oppression of minorities, or the general betterment of human society. There is barely a mention of such general topics as science, religion, labor, industry, politics, or war. The entries are apolitical to a degree that may scandalize some of our young people today, but only those, I hasten to surmise, who remain willfully ignorant of what the creative process consists of. For these entries should not be taken to mean that James was not interested in the subjects which they eschew. Any reader of his letters and essays knows to the contrary. The notebooks were rigidly — and necessarily — confined to those sparks which James knew from experience could be kindled into his particular brand of fiction. As a writer, he had no use for any others.

It is very difficult for nonwriters to comprehend this. Every novelist is familiar with the tiresome friend who has a "true story" which is simply waiting to be converted into fiction. The friend never realizes that the most, if not the only, interesting thing about his story is precisely the fact that it is true — which quality it would inevitably lose when fictionalized. But over and beyond this is the more important fact that the writer can use only his own spark or germ or *donnée* or whatever he chooses to call it. The friend may possibly suggest one to the writer in the course of his chatter, but this will usually be in some odd, irrelevant part of his story. The writer, however, learns to recognize his spark when it flashes before his eyes — whether in his own fantasies or from the conversation around him or in the books he reads or in something he has merely glimpsed — and without questioning its importance to the rest of the world he seizes it for his very own. Why should he care if it seems trivial to others? Only *he* knows what he can make of it. And only by what he makes of it can he be judged — unless, like James, he is unwary enough to leave notebooks for the unknowing to sniff at. James made a bonfire of all his private papers, but he kept the notebooks to the end. After all, he might at any time have had need of them.

"London in November, and Mr Henry James in London: . . .
It was, therefore, not without something of a shock that he, in this
to him so very congenial atmosphere, now perceived that a vision
of the hand which he had, at a venture, held up within an inch or
so of his eyes was, with an almost awful clarity
being adumbrated . . ." (Beerbohm, 1907)

His relation with his genius or muse is delightful to follow through the entries, though some might find it embarrassingly intimate. Here are a few examples, taken at random over a period of years, which show him almost crooning to himself:

The little things to do will all come to me . . . I hold out my arms to them, I gather them in. *À l'oeuvre, mon bon, à l'oeuvre — roide!* . . . I take up, in other words, this little blessed, this sacred small, 'ciphering' pen that has stood me in such stead often already, and I call down on it the benediction of the old days, I invoke the aid of the old patience and passion and piety. . . . Ah, things swim before me, *caro mio*, and I only need to sit tight, to keep my place and fix my eyes, to see them float past me in the current into which I can cast my little net and make my little haul. . . . *Causons, causons, mon bon* — oh celestial, soothing, sanctifying process, with all the high sane forces of the sacred time fighting through it, on my side! . . . I seem to emerge from these recent bad days — the fruit of blind accident — and the prospect clears and flushes, and my poor blest old Genius pats me so admirably and lovingly on the back that I turn, I screw around, and bend my lips to passionately, in my gratitude, kiss its hand.

It was not, actually, in his notebooks but in his preface to *The Spoils of Poynton* that James most precisely described the process of receiving an idea for a tale. Here he stressed the "minuteness" of the "precious particle," the casual hint dropped unwittingly by a dinner partner: "Such is the interesting truth about the stray suggestion, the wandering word, the vague echo, at touch of which the novelist's imagination winces as at the prick of some sharp point: its virtue is all in its needle-like quality, the power to penetrate as finely as possible."

But is this all? Is the writer at the mercy of such pinpricks? Can he never deliberately engage on a great subject? I doubt that he can — successfully. Yet James himself felt the need of just this. In 1893 we find him inscribing this pious precept in his notebook: "I want to do something fine — a strong, large, important human episode, something that brings into play character and sincerity and passion; something that marches like a drama. A truce to all subjects that are not superior!" What writer has not felt that? And what good has it ever done him? He must wait, as James waited, for his *données* to come. *They* will determine, at least in part, the superiority or inferiority of the subject that grows out of them. What is most rewarding in a study of the notebooks is that one begins to make out in James's initial inspirations the ultimate quality of the tale which they engender. I realize that I am now coming perilously close to the argument that a writer is the slave of his vagrant imagination, but let us take some examples.

I start by making the point that if all, or most, of James's originating literary germs may seem trivial to the nonwriter, *not* all, or even most, of them were capable of being developed, even by James himself, into stories of the first rank. He recognized at once the kind of story that he could write. But he did not distinguish between those kernels that he could develop into first-rate James and those that he could develop only into second- or third-rate James. I suggest that where the imagined or suggested factual situation does not of necessity imply the existence of at least one strongly individual character — where the facts, in other words, could drape themselves over a wide range of diverse human beings — the resulting story is minor James. If, on the other hand, a vivid and special character seems to spring inevitably from the *donnée*, a major James work is in the making. The situation, for example, of a bald woman buying a wig fits any female who has lost her hair. But what of the situation of the bald woman who refuses to buy one?

In the following examples of stories suggested by my two types of situations, I am assuming that the reader will agree with my classifications of "minor" and "major." I start with minor stories inspired by situations in which a strongly individual character is not implicit.

"The Path of Duty" arose from this entry:

> The story was told of young Lord Stafford, son of the Duke of Sutherland. It appears he has been for years in love with Lady Grosvenor whom he knew before her marriage to Lord G. He had no expectation of being able to marry her, however, her husband being a young, robust man of his own age, etc. Yielding to family pressure on the subject of taking a wife, he offered his hand to a young, charming, innocent girl, the daughter of Lord Rosslyn. He was gratefully accepted, and the engagement was announced. Suddenly, a very short time after this, and without anyone's expecting it, Lord Grosvenor dies . . .

When James came to write the story, the entire interest, mild enough, was inevitably centered in the situation. The characters have only enough individuality to fulfill their given roles.

"The Marriages" originated from another social situation. James learned in a letter that one "Sir J. R." was about to marry the "Dowager Lady T." and that the former's daughter had sourly observed that it was "simply forty years of her mother's life wiped out." "There is a little drama here," James records. But in writing the tale, he discovered that Adela Chart's objections to her father's remarriage had to be intensified — to make a story — to the point of turning her into a hysteric. The tale ends as a clinical case history. And the following idea for "The Solution" suggests not a character but a simpleton, which is how the story came out:

Say, indefatigable alchemist,
Melts not the very moral of our scene,
Curls it not off in vapour from between
Those lips that labour with conspicuous twist?
Your fine eyes, blurred like arc-lamps in a mist,
Immensely glare; yet glimmerings intervene,
So that your May-Be and Your-Might-Have-Been
Leave us still plunging for your genuine gist.

How different from Sir Arthur Conan Doyle—
As clear as water, and as smooth as oil,
And no jot knowing of what Maisie knew.
Flushed with the sunset air of roseate Rye,
You stand, marmoreal darling of the few,
Lord of the troubled Speech and single Eye.

Mightn't I do something fairly good with that idea I made a note of long ago — the idea of the young man on whom some companions impose the idea that he has so committed himself with regard to a girl that he must propose to her — he is bound in honour — and who does propose, credulously, *naïvement*, to do the right thing, and is eagerly accepted, having money and being something of a *parti*.

One of the more artificial and less humane of James's longer tales, "Lord Beaupré," had its genesis in this entry, which should have carried with it its own warning:

An *idée de comédie* came to me vaguely the other day on the subject of the really terrible situation of the young man, in England, who is a great *parti* — the really formidable assault of the mothers, and the *filles à marier*. I don't see, quite, my comedy in it yet — but I do see a little tale of about this kind. — A young nobleman — or only (perhaps better) commoner of immense wealth, feels himself, on the eve of the London Season, in such real discomfort and peril that he makes a compact with a girl he has known for years, and likes, to see him through the wood by allowing it to be supposed and announced, that they are engaged.

What sort of man would ask a young woman to pretend to be his fiancée? Only a fatuous egoist. Perhaps here the

Left: a caricature Beerbohm drew for Edmund Gosse in 1908, when the two composed alternate lines of this sonnet:

Say, indefatigable alchemist,
Melts not the very moral of your scene,
Curls it not off in vapour from between
Those lips that labour with conspicuous twist?
Your fine eyes, blurred like arc-lamps in a mist,
Immensely glare; yet glimmerings intervene,
So that your May-Be and your Might-Have-Been
Leave us still plunging for your genuine gist.

How different from Sir Arthur Conan Doyle —
As clear as water, and as smooth as oil,
And no jot knowing of what Maisie knew.
Flushed with the sunset air of roseate Rye,
You stand, marmoreal darling of the few,
Lord of the troubled Speech and single Eye.

character *is* inherent in the situation, but the character is too vapid to carry a tale of such length. Similarly, "The Wheel of Time" requires two men who are utterly repulsed by women who are not utterly beautiful. Can one not see the ultimate mildness of the story in the following genesis?

Little subject suggested by some talk last night with Lady Shrewsbury, at dinner at Lady Lindsay's: about the woman who has been very ugly in youth and been slighted and snubbed for her ugliness, and who, as very frequently — or at least sometimes — happens with plain girls, has become much better-looking, almost handsome in middle life, and later — and with this improvement in appearance, charming, at any rate, and attractive — so that the later years are, practically, her advantage, her compensation, her *revanche*. Idea of such a woman who meets, in such a situation, a man who, in her youth, has slighted and snubbed her . . .

"Miss Gunton of Poughkeepsie" could hardly grow into anything of much more substance than its germ, the idea of an American girl with the *idée fixe* that the mother of her fiancé, a proud Roman princess, should write to her first. And the subject of "Glasses" proved capable of little greater development than the following:

A very pretty, a very beautiful little woman, devoted to her beauty, which she cherishes, prizing and rejoicing in it more than in anything on earth — is threatened, becomes indeed absolutely afflicted, with a malady of the eyes which she goes to see oculists about. She has had it for a long time, and has been told that she must wear spectacles of a certain kind, a big strong, unbecoming kind, with a *bar* across them, etc. — if she wishes to preserve her sight.

My last example of minor tales springing from characterless plots is "Fordham Castle," the fantastic story of homely old Abel Taker who gives out that he is dead and consents to live in obscurity under a false name so that his socially ambitious wife may continue her climb to the peak of Gotham and even advantageously remarry. This absurd little confection was suggested to James by the comment of a friend as they left a drawing-room tea at the American Embassy about "the American phenomenon" of the social suppression of parents.

I turn now to situations which from their very genesis involve characters of strength or interest. Are not the couple in "The Liar," the charming, compulsively driven Colonel Capadose and his tragic wife, implicit in this plot:

> One might write a tale (very short) about a woman married to a man of the most amiable character who is a tremendous, though harmless, liar. She is very intelligent, a fine, quiet, high, pure nature, and she has to sit by and hear him romance . . . But there comes a day when he tells a very big lie which she has — for reasons to be related — to adopt, to reinforce. To save him from exposure, in a word, she has to lie herself.

The antecedent of "Greville Fane" came from Thackeray's daughter, Mrs. Ritchie. She told James that Trollope had had a plan to bring up his son to be a novelist and that she and her husband were adopting the same for their daughter. This suggested to James (possibly as a combination of Ouida with Mrs. Ritchie herself) "the figure of a weary battered labourer in the field of fiction attempting to carry out this project with a child and meeting, by the irony of fate, the strangest discomfiture."

Once the figure and situation of Greville Fane had been conceived, James could easily clothe her in a story of his own devising, i.e., one that did not have any apparent relation to the germ. Indeed, it was better if the germ were small. Let us take "The Real Thing," which sprang from an incident related to James by George du Maurier: "The lady and gentleman who called upon him with a word from Frith [a well-known illustrator], an oldish, faded, ruined pair — he an officer in the army — who unable to turn a penny in any other way, were trying to find employment as models." Nothing else was needed. We see James's mind going quickly to work as the entry progresses, and on the very next page he seizes his "gimmick": that the old couple are less qualified to pose for what they themselves really are — the Colonel and his lady — than a couple of professional models who have no inside knowledge of high life. "What I wish to represent is the baffled, ineffectual, incompetent character of their attempt, and how it illustrates once again the everlasting English amateurishness — the way superficial, untrained, unprofessional effort goes to the wall when confronted with trained, competitive, intelligent, *qualified* art — in whatever line it may be a question of."

At this point in the entry James recognizes the perfection of his germ and the completeness of its working out, and he renders devout homage to his muse. It is a unique glimpse into the creative process: "It is out of *that* element that my little action and movement must come; and now I begin to see just how — as one always *does* — Glory be to the Highest — when one begins to look at a thing hard and straight and seriously — to fix it — as I am so sadly lax and desultory about doing. What subjects I should find — for *everything* — if I could only achieve this more as a habit!"

No story is more elaborately thought out in all the notebooks than *The Spoils of Poynton*, no subject looked at more "straightly and seriously," yet the original conception is contained in a few lines, an anecdote told James at dinner by a Mrs. Anstruther-Thompson:

Some young laird, in Scotland, inherited, by the death of his father, a large place filled with valuable things — pictures, old china, etc., etc. His mother was still living, and had always lived, in this rich old house, in which she took pride and delight. After the death of her husband she was at first left unmolested there by her son, though there was a small dower-house (an inferior and contracted habitation) attached to the property in another part of the country. But the son married — married promptly and young — and went down with his wife to take possession — possession *exclusive*, of course — according to English custom. On doing so he found that pictures and other treasures were absent — and had been removed by his mother.

It might be argued that this scenario is a situation without a necessarily implied central character, but I maintain that Mrs. Gereth, imperious, indomitable, of the grandest manner and most superb taste, springs naturally from this glimpse of the young laird's mother.

What is perhaps the greatest of James's novels, *The Wings of the Dove*, originated in the simplest of all his fictional germs:

Isn't perhaps something to be made of the idea that came to me some time ago and that I have not hitherto made any note of — the little idea of the situation of some young creature (it seems to me preferably a woman, but of this I'm not sure), who, at 20, on the threshold of a life that has seemed boundless, is suddenly condemned to death (by consumption, heart-disease, or whatever) by the voice of the physician? She learns that she has but a short time to live, and she rebels, she is terrified, she cries out in her anguish, her tragic young despair. She is in love with life . . .

Now where is the character of Milly Theale in all this? Is there anything but the fact of dying? James is not even initially sure of the creature's sex. But note that the pronouns are all feminine. It seems to me that the exquisite pathos of Milly is inherent in this sketch, that one can draw out of it the beginnings of her beautiful fortitude and delicate generosity. It is a case of the character being born with her plight. Seeing the stricken creature and feeling pity for her, the observing artist tends to endow her with all the qualities which will make her extinction the more cruel. Then what of "Glasses"? Why does one not deduce a fine character from the plight of a beautiful girl condemned to wear disfiguring spectacles? Because the menace is to her vanity, not to her life. Milly Theale would still have been a princess in double lenses.

The difference in the nature of the heroine's plight in "Glasses" and in *The Wings of the Dove* may be obvious, but it is immensely important. A trivial subject will cheapen the work of the greatest artist. Timon in *Timon of Athens* rants at the universe as magnificently as does King Lear, but he fails as a tragic hero because he has brought misfortune on his own neck by throwing his money around among friends whom the audience can immediately spot as untrustworthy. Timon is an ass, and once a protagonist has shown himself an ass, he can never be elevated. King Lear may seem on the brink of asininity in the beginning of his tragedy when he disinherits Cordelia and exiles Kent, but he is old, very old, and his own children are in league against him. He is pitiable.

In the finest of his short stories James envisioned factual situations which suggested characters with a single dominant trait. Indeed, these stories are primarily concerned with the trait. The character is individualized by having a "quirk" — almost to the exclusion of other characteristics — and being to this extent a bit of a fanatic. Thus in "The Altar of the Dead" James imagined a man, Stransom, "whose noble and beautiful religion is the worship of the Dead." Stransom "cherishes for the silent, for the patient, the unreproaching dead, a tenderness in which all his private need of something, not of this world, to cherish, to be pious to, to make the object of a donation, finds a sacred, and almost a secret, expression."

Similarly, for "The Middle Years," James saw an old writer, Dencombe, in this fashion: "He is the man who has developed late, obstructedly, with difficulty, has needed all life to learn, to see his way, to collect material, and now feels that if he can only have another life to make use of this clear start, he can show what he is really capable of."

And finally, in what I consider the greatest of all James's short stories, "The Beast in the Jungle," the kernel came in this simple sentence: "Meanwhile there is something else — a very tiny *fantaisie* probably — in [the] small notion that comes to me of a man haunted by the fear, more and more, throughout life, that *something will happen to him*; he doesn't quite know what."

The notebooks contain many instances of abortive germs: ideas that James never afterwards developed or that he developed and destroyed. Armed with the distinction that I have made between characterless and charactered situations, I cannot resist the game of predicting which of these abortive germs might have grown into second-rate tales and which, first-rate. I submit two examples. Here is one that I think would have become, if developed, one of James's hollower tales, which I shall call "The Imitator": "The idea of such an imitation — of the person making it — operating as a source of disenchantment (through accentuation of the points least liked) to a person deeply interested in the model — in the individual imitated. More concretely a woman, say, is in love with the great artist (poet, soldier, orator, actor — whatever), A." As James proceeds to embroider his theme, we learn that the woman meets the imitator, B, who falls in love with her. B then imitates A in such a way as to disillusion the woman with A. When next she sees A, she flees from him in horror. The imitation has been fatal. But it has also been fatal for B. B has a sincere admiration for his defeated rival which is what makes his imitation so profound. Thereafter the woman sees A's least lovable characteristics not only in A but in B. I suspect that in the finished story cleverness would have taken the place of feeling.

On the other hand here is an 1894 entry suggested by Stopford Brooke: "The man (*à propos* of S.B.) who has become afraid of himself when alone — vaguely afraid of his own company, personality, disposition, character, presence, fate; so that he plunges into society, noise, sound, the sense of diversion, distraction, protection, connected with the presence of others, etc." I can well imagine this idea developed into another "Beast in the Jungle."

The most unpredictable thing in James's genius as sensed in the notebooks is the quality of the stories which are inspired by his passion for symmetry. He dearly loved an equation; he eyed with fondness balances and compensations. Sometimes this resulted in a fantastic but fascinating story like "The Private Life," where Lord Mellifont, who has only a public life, no private one, and who actually disappears — ceases to exist — when alone, is balanced by Clare Vawdrey, the writer who has no public life but an intense private one and who becomes a greater presence in solitude. But it could also produce what to me (and despite Leon Edel's persuasive defense) still remains the most dismal of all James's fictions, *The Sacred Fount.* There the characters, like vampires, feed on each other. A young man who marries an older wife actually withers as she becomes rejuvenated, and a clever woman in love with a dull man actually loses her wit as he gains it. What could save James's symmetry from such artificiality was its combination with a situation implying a strong, interesting character. This was the case with *The Ambassadors*, the perfect Jamesian novel.

The character of the hero, Lambert Strether, was suggested to James by Jonathan Sturges. The latter related to him how, once in Whistler's Paris studio, the old novelist William Dean Howells had laid his hand paternally on his shoulder and delivered the following exhortation: "Oh, you are young, you are young — be glad of it; be glad of it and *live*. Live all you can: it's a mistake not to. It doesn't so much matter what you do — but live. This place makes it all come over me. I see it now. I haven't done so — and now I'm old. It's too late. It has gone past me — I've lost it. You have time. You are young. Live!" It didn't make a particle of difference to James that Howells's own life might have seemed rich and full by most standards. What he seized on in a flash for his own purposes was the peculiar vision that Howells had of himself — and Lambert Strether was born. Strether has all Howells's famed kindness and benignity; he has all his intelligence and compassion, but, unlike the Howells of reality, he *has* wasted his life. He is fifty-five and alone in the world, with nothing to show for his dreary years in a small New England town but a dead wife and a dead son and the editorship of a small, futile New England quarterly supported by a rich and formidable widow whom he is almost resigned to marrying. When Paris is spread before his dazzled eyes, his old values fall.

The plot which James constructs around Strether is of a perfect symmetry. Strether is sent out from Woollett to bring back Mrs. Newsome's errant son Chad, but Strether and Chad change places in the course of their tale.

Strether falls in love with Paris and at last comprehends that the young man has been improved and not corrupted by Madame de Vionnet, his French mistress. Chad, on the other hand, is charmed by his mother's ambassador and finds him a pleasant reintroduction to a Woollett life to which he fully intends to return when through with a liaison that has already begun to pall. In the beginning, Strether is the limited American with blinkers, and Chad the polished cosmopolite. In the end Strether's heart is beating to the pulse of all that is finest in the French capital, and Chad is beginning to reveal to us that, after all, he is not too good for a Woollett world. Strether's mission has been to bring Chad home; he ends by urging him to stay. Chad's original problem (to Woollett eyes) has been his fatal enchainment to Paris; his final one is how to break away from his mistress and go home without offending Strether. The moral has become the immoral, and vice versa. Woollett and Paris remain eternally the same, but Strether and Chad change allegiances. To me there is nothing more beautiful in all fiction than the way in which this is made to happen.

The Early Stories

In 1878 James published "Daisy Miller" and became
famous. He was thirty-five, a pleasant age for success,
but he had been putting out stories regularly for a
decade and a half. From "A Tragedy of Error" in 1864 to
"Four Meetings" in 1877 he published thirty stories and
the short novel *Watch and Ward*. Yet except for three of
these, "A Passionate Pilgrim," "The Madonna of the Future," and "Madame de Mauves," none would be apt to be
included in any discriminating anthology of American
short stories. James received early recognition as a writer
of talent, but there was little in his first phase to
foreshadow, even to the discerning, the future author of
The Ambassadors.

The early tales have been widely, and I think justifiably,
attributed to the school of Hawthorne. Many of them have
the characteristics of fables. The background, whether it
be New York, Boston, Newport, or, more generally, "New
England," is sketched in with a minimum of detail, and the
characters are no more developed than need be to per-

form their individual roles. The plots, with their turns and twists, are in some instances all-important: the long story "Osborne's Revenge," for example, depends entirely on Osborne's misconception of Henrietta Congreve's treatment of his friend Graham. The reader's interest is usually held by skillful narration, and there is frequently a little thrill of satisfaction at the "gimmick" that ends the tale. The stories, with their stripped, simplified Hawthornesque settings, have charm, but they lack in general Hawthorne's depth of feeling.

A slow (or at least not meteoric) literary start may frequently be the fate of writers who are essentially scenically minded. The mature James viewed the world and its people with a painter's eye, and he came to see his plots enacted, as on a stage. The individual situation, the drama of given human beings, was ultimately everything to him. In order to convey his vivid, overflowing sense of his imagined set and characters he had first to develop his descriptive powers, and this was the story of his life as both man and artist. Writers who depend more on the direct impact of some striking aspect of their subject material are apt to obtain earlier recognition. Theodore Dreiser, who wanted to abolish poverty, Emily Brontë, who burned with a fierce inner fire, Norman Mailer, who was obsessed with the terrible war in which he had just fought, are examples of novelists who attained maturity in their first books. For James the process was to be lifelong.

For all his deep concern with his artistic future, he did not, in the beginning of his career, foresee the kind of novelist that he was ultimately to become. The most notable characteristic of such of the early stories as have American settings is the absence of descriptive detail. Like Hawthorne's, they are as simple and bare as modern stage sets, with the interest all focused on the characters who, as creatures in a fable, seem to exist in no specified time or place. Here and there we may get a glimpse of a patch of beach or a shingled summer cottage which may briefly suggest the simple, pre-Gilded Age Newport which James had loved to paint as a young man under the kindly tutelage of John La Farge, but for the most part the houses and hotels might be houses and hotels anywhere. The most extreme example of this is *Watch and Ward* in which there is not a single paragraph to differentiate the central locale, Boston, from that of New York, the city to which the major characters migrate in the last chapters. When one thinks of the magnificent sketches that James was to do for the "hub of the universe" a decade and a half later in *The Bostonians*, one wonders how it was possible for the younger writer to throw away such opportunities.

It sprang partly, no doubt, from a feeling that the American background was scarcely worth putting in. It was too bare, too poor, too scrappy. But as soon as a character in one of these early tales goes to Europe, James immediately pulls out his paint box. Nora, the ward of *Watch and Ward*, is sent to Rome for a year's "finishing" with the sophisticated widow Mrs. Keith. Formerly a rather silent girl, she becomes at once volubly communicative, and the portion of the novel that contains her long letters home could be lifted out with no loss to the story and inserted into James's first travel book, *Transatlantic Sketches*. It was a remarkable perversity in Nora's creator to make her describe at such length the city where she does *not* live and where no action occurs.

There has been some academic interest in recent years in three of these early stories that deal, albeit indirectly, with the Civil War, but I ascribe this to the passionate concern of American scholars with the question of James's attitude toward his native land. I do not share this interest. It seems perfectly obvious to me that James never studied the United States with any depth until his American tour in 1904 when he was sixty, the fruits of which he incorporated into that remarkable volume *The American Scene*. As a young man I take it that he was utterly absorbed in England, France, and Italy. He solved the literary problem of how to use as his characters the people he knew best from birth by the simple expedient of moving his fellow nationals to Europe. A novelist is always a bit of a monologist: his characters are largely extensions of himself. James was an American who preferred to live in Europe, so his fiction became peopled with expatriates.

The better of the early tales, therefore, at least to my way of thinking, are those which are most full of the romance of Europe, those where we most intensely feel the young American pilgrim "reeling and moaning" through the streets of the older civilization. "The Sweetheart of M. Briseux" comes brilliantly alive when the hungry young French painter, full of the sense of his great future and miserable present, electrifies the English girl whom he finds in a Paris studio by converting her fiancé's wretched portrait of herself into a masterpiece. The episode costs her her marriage, but one feels that it was worth it. A day's exposure to genius has marked her, and she can never return to the commonplace. The story, set in the 1830s, might be dealing with the young Ingres, for James, even as a young man, had the feeling that he had come to Europe, glorious as he found it, almost too late, and he loved to imagine how it must have been in his childhood or even earlier. In "Adina," this passage gives me a vivid sense of nostalgia for the pretourist Rome of William Wetmore

Story: "You remember those days of early winter, when the sun is as strong as that of a New England June, and the bare, purple-drawn slopes and hollows lie bathed in the yellow light of Italy. On such a day, Scrope and I mounted our horses in the grassy terrace before St John Lateran, and rode away across the broad meadows over which the Claudian Aqueduct drags its slow length — stumbling and lapsing here and there, as it goes, beneath the burden of the centuries."

"Gabrielle de Bergerac" is an early experiment with a French background. It is precisely situated in time and place: a French province in the eighteenth century, with a fine old château, a noble family of great pride and small means, a passionate tutor with romantic revolutionary ideals, and a beautiful girl who defies her background to respond to them. It is an exquisite sketch, delicate and sad, a charming exercise in the genre of *Henry Esmond*, but James considered afterwards that he had no business intruding upon eras which he could not know at firsthand, or very nearly, and he never did so again until the unfinished *The Sense of the Past*, which is really more a tour de force than a historical novel, dealing as it does with a modern man who transcends time to visit his ancestors. I am of the opinion that James was wrong to eschew historical fiction and that his sense of the eighteenth century was as finely developed as Thackeray's, but there is no arguing with a writer's choice of subject.

"A Passionate Pilgrim," whose American hero comes to England for the first time as a dying man to have one long, deep, belated bittersweet gulp of an atmosphere for which he has yearned his whole lifetime, shows James at last in full possession of his great descriptive powers. The story suffers from a certain ambivalence about the passionate pilgrim's character — is he a silly ass or a romantic hero? — but the English countryside is evoked with lyrical effect. All James had to do now was to reperceive his native land. He was soon to do it.

"Madame de Mauves" is the only product of this period in which I can clearly make out the future author of *The Portrait of a Lady*, though I am not quite happy with the two principal characters. It seems to me that the Baron de Mauves would never have experienced an emotion strong enough to drive him to suicide, and I cannot determine just what it is that James is saying about his wife. Is she a foolishly romantic girl who turns perversely frigid when she finds that the world is not the fairy tale that she has imagined it? Or is she, like Isabel Archer, the finest type of American woman, something too exquisite for an ancient and corrupted civilization to appreciate? But I forget my questions in the beautiful mood and setting of the story. The silent greenness of the countryside at Saint-Germain fits perfectly with the calm resignation of the ineluctable heroine, and I sense that the nervous agitations of her foolish would-be lover, Longmore, and of her malicious sister-in-law are hardly more than light breaths of wind in a hot summer day.

To make a last distinction between these early stories and James's later fiction, I point to the difference in the character of the narrator in those tales where this device is used. James came to distrust it as tending to promote looseness in a story. He never used it in a novel and used it diminishingly in the later tales. Where he did use it, the narrator was apt to be like James himself, removed from the immediate action, an observer, dispassionate, only mildly involved, almost sexless, like the man-about-town in "Brooksmith" and "Greville Fane." But in these early

stories James still liked to imagine himself as directly par-
ticipating. His narrators are engaged with life at firsthand:
the "I" of "Guest's Confession," a "stoutish, blondish, indolent, amiable, rather gorgeous young fellow," pursues a
reluctant young woman with ardor and ultimate success;
the "I" of "At Isella" helps a young woman fleeing from a
tyrannical husband to escape over the Italian border; the
"I" of "My Friend Bingham" goes shooting sea gulls with a
companion who shoots and kills a child by mistake; the "I"
of "The Ghostly Rental" enters a haunted house alone at
dusk to penetrate the mysteries of an alleged spirit. But
these "involved" narrators add little enough to the plots in
which they are involved. The blood which their successors
lost was beneficially added to their stories. To me, everything that preceded "Daisy Miller," with the exception of
"Madame de Mauves," has the air of a literary exercise.
But, of course, they are the literary exercises of a titan.

Roderick Hudson and *The American*

James's first two long novels are pleasant mixtures of the romantic and the realistic. They have a verve and a swing that is not generally associated with his later work. Indeed, they contain chapters that border on the melodramatic. I am always in a quandary in advising people unfamiliar with James where they should start. If I suggest *The American*, they may love it and then forever after be disappointed, looking in vain for the wicked Bellegardes and their sinister plots.

Roderick Hudson, the lesser of these two novels, has a delightful first half. The hero starts out as a Byronic romantic character, beautiful to look at, with a high, brave forehead and abundant black hair, and an ambition as violent as it is naive. Roderick is so intense that he seems ready to explode into small pieces all over the quiet town of Northampton, Massachusetts, where his genius is initially confined. One feels that Rowland Mallet, his impresario, far from exposing him to temptation by taking him to Rome, is getting him out of his hometown just in time.

Roderick's emotional effusions and his wild confidence in his own star succeed in being charming — at least in the early part of the novel — and Christina Light with her brilliant looks and high style seems to be just the romantic heroine to sweep him off his feet in the ancient city of the Caesars.

But at this point things begin to change. Christina Light is seen to be a complex character. She has been corrupted by a mother whose values are purely mercenary, but she clings fiercely to a sense of personal integrity which manifests itself in a candor of conversation that is often synonymous with simple bad manners. Christina toys with the idea of throwing over an immensely rich Neapolitan prince for Roderick, who, though penniless, has already become a noted artist, but she is made to stick to her great marriage by her mother's desperate expedient of threatening to publish the fact that she is a bastard. Just why this threat should be so fatal to Christina's plans to elope with an artist to whom convention is nonsense is never quite clear, but the effect of her change on Roderick is catastrophic. He suffers a kind of nervous breakdown, abandons his work, and finally meets his death in a mountain fall that may or may not be suicide.

Of course, one can see the kind of impassioned, impetuous, emotionally unstable artist that James had in mind, a man subject to giddy heights and despairing depths, a visionary who is always in search of the unattainable and who derives little satisfaction from even his finest accomplishments in the immediate past. But just what James means us to learn from Roderick's sorry case is harder to tell. Was Rowland wrong to have taken him from home and exposed him to the temptations of Rome? Would Roderick not have tired even more quickly of his subdued betrothed, Mary Garland, had he remained in Northampton? And are we to suppose that Roderick would have been "all right" had he never met Christina? Is *she* the villainess, pure and simple?

I suppose that what troubles me is that the symptoms of Roderick's mental malady are described so graphically that I cannot help seeing his case in psychological terms that did not exist in 1875 and that would not, in any event, have interested James. This is true also of Olive Chancellor's lesbianism in *The Bostonians*. But James was concerned with Roderick the sculptor, not Roderick the patient. He was presumably trying to express, in a kind of fable, the fate of the artist who cannot learn to discipline himself and live in the civilized world. Rowland, obviously, is conceived in terms of opposites to his protégé; he is all kindness and self-control and common sense, with no least spark of artistic genius. Roderick, on the other hand, is totally selfish — as only an artist can be — and totally at the mercy of his impulses. When the impulse happens to be to work, it obliges him to create a great statue, but when it is to drink or run after a married woman, it is equally irresistible. So what can any of the other characters, Rowland, Mary, or Mrs. Hudson, do about him? Nothing!

Perhaps James was writing a determinist novel: given Roderick and his temperament, then Roderick must go to the devil. But this is never made quite clear. Christina Light plays too baffling a role. Obviously, she fascinated James, for he resurrected her in *The Princess Casamassima* where she is even more baffling. The difficulty with Christina's position in *Roderick Hudson* is that she is so unusual a woman as to seem to put Roderick under an unusual test, even for an artist. Had she been a more ordinary female, their love affair might not have destroyed him. But if that is the case, then Roderick's going to the devil is simply a piece of bad luck. It seems to me that what Christina Light actually *is* in the novel, i.e., the most dazzling woman in Rome, is what Roderick the artist should have perversely insisted on seeing in some more commonplace woman. What is flat in the novel is to have the sculptor's Egeria exactly what the sculptor imagines her to be. This is where the romantic and the realist approaches do not mix. For although Roderick's mental and physical decline results from a Byronic passion, James describes it with the same precision that the Goncourt brothers used for their heroine's fatal ailment in *Renée Mauperin*. It puts the novel off balance.

The American is certainly not a determinist novel. It is almost a Gothic tale. It stands by itself in James's work, and for what it is, it is perfect. An Andromeda waiting for the dragon, the lovely Claire de Cintré is walled up alternately in a dark old *hôtel* in the Faubourg Saint-Germain and in a dark old crumbling castle in Poitiers, jealously guarded by her splendid tyrant of a mother, the Marquise de Belle-garde, and an older brother, Urbain, whose icy manners and poltroonish character would elicit hisses in a melo-drama. The hero from the American West, Christopher Newman, charges onto the scene, honest, frank, strong, unimpressed and unafraid, determined to storm Claire's dusky redoubts and carry her off to a brave New World where she will be able at last to breathe and live. But the forces of darkness prevail in the end, and Claire flees both her family and her lover to incarcerate herself for life in the strictest of convents. Newman, who has meanwhile dis-covered that Madame de Bellegarde has murdered her husband, threatens the old hag with exposure, but when he realizes that even this will not release his beloved, he philosophically destroys his incriminating evidence and presumably returns to America.

It is a wonderful, colorful, thrilling tale. The visits of Newman to the Bellegarde's *hôtel*, his verbal spars with the indomitable, scathing, uncompromising marquise, his friendship with her charming, philandering younger son, Valentin (who, true to the anachronism of his hopeless social position, dies in a duel), his passionate pleas to Claire to abandon her living death make of *The American* an opera in prose. It is for this reason that I have not included it in my chapter on the "international situation." For the book does not really deal with an international situation, any more than does *Madama Butterfly*.

In the first place, had an international theme been dominant, the Bellegardes would not have backed out of their agreement to give Claire to an American millionaire. They would not have been so violently disturbed at his easy manners (which were really very good manners) at their reception in his honor. It was a clever stroke on James's part to make the old marquise the daughter of an English Catholic earl, thus adding to the arrogance of the French legitimist nobility the intransigeance of the Jacobite peerage, but even so, if she had been capable of committing a murder to catch her daughter's first rich husband, she would have been capable of shrugging her shoulders to catch a second. James came in time to realize this, and in his preface to the novel in the New York Edition he admitted that the Bellegardes in life would have "jumped" at his rich American.

Secondly, the Bellegardes are really more villains than they are either French or English. When a writer introduces murder, he brings in a subject that dwarfs all others.

The melodrama of *The American* is excellent melodrama, but it can hardly survive analysis. Why was old Monsieur de Cintré such a catch for the great Bellegardes as to justify homicide? Why would a creature of such character and resolution as Claire is depicted to be — and a widow to boot — immediately give up her betrothed at the capricious command of an arbitrary old mother whom she knows to be both capricious and arbitrary? And isn't Christopher Newman himself something less than the spokesman of Yankeeland in being so anxious to find a bride in the Almanach de Gotha?

So Newman versus the wicked Bellegardes is nearer to a cloak-and-dagger drama than it is to a contemporary study of international mores. There are moments when the marquise and her son seem to have been worked up out of the early romantic Balzac, with a dash of the elder Dumas. And yet the James of the middle period, the James of his own *comédie humaine*, is already making his appearance. There is nothing in the least romantic about Mrs. Tristram. This sharp, bright, frustrated little expatriate, married to a fop whom she despises and whom she despises herself for having married, gets such amusement as she can out of her limited life on the sidelines by making trenchant observations about Parisian society to the carefully noting Newman. When she meets the Marquise de Bellegarde, it is as if a character from parlor comedy has encountered one from grand opera, and James wisely tells us about it at secondhand. We are not surprised to learn that Mrs. Tristram promptly sacrifices her husband to get in a dig at the idleness of the Bellegardes. When the marquise inquires contemptuously the nature of Mr. Tristram's "trade," his wife retorts: "My husband, Madame la

Marquise, belongs to that unfortunate class of persons who have no profession and no business, and do very little good in the world." This is worthy of Henrietta Stackpole in *The Portrait of a Lady*, but it almost disintegrates the opera. For sheer entertainment there is nothing in the Jamesian canon like *The American*.

Washington Square
and "The Aspern Papers"

*W*ashington Square* has for so long been beloved by almost all readers — particularly those who turn away with a sniff from what they like to call the "overwrought effusions" of the late Jamesian style — that it may be profitable to consider why it failed to please the most discriminating reader of all: its author. When James was assembling and revising his lifework for the great Scribner edition, he decided to omit the little story of Catherine Sloper and Morris Townsend that he had written twenty-seven years before. It was apparently too simple a fare for his later and more refined vision. But to other readers it was as if *A Midsummer Night's Dream* had been dropped from the First Folio.

The publication of *Washington Square* in 1880 and of *The Portrait of a Lady* in 1881 marks the beginning of the Balzac period of James's career. He was thirty-seven, and the long, self-conscious apprenticeship, which had involved experimental residence in Paris and Italy and the cultivation of almost every major French or English writer, was behind him. He had settled permanently in London, where he had conquered the social world that was to provide him with such copious material, and he thought that at last he saw his way clear to becoming what he had described to his brother William as a "sufficiently great man." His "human comedy" was to do this for him.

We know from the notebooks that the plot was derived from the story that Fanny Kemble told him of her brother's heartless jilting of an heiress, but Balzac's *Eugénie Grandet*, with its beautifully constructed atmosphere of patience and waste emanating from the broken heart of a dull, good woman, caught between an egocentric father and a mercenary lover, is still the literary ancestor. It is also possible that James had read a little-known novel of Anthony Trollope, *Sir Harry Hotspur of Humblethwaite*, which had appeared just ten years before. In this sad tale, Emily Hotspur pines away and dies when her lover abandons his suit in return for the settlement of his debts by her father. But unlike Catherine Sloper, Emily ultimately agrees with her father that he is acting for the best.

In all these novels the fathers are correct in their estimates of the suitors' mercenary motives, but they differ widely in their attitudes toward their daughters. Balzac's father is so obsessed with his avarice as to have no interest at all in his daughter's plight. Sir Harry Hotspur, on the other hand, is a totally loving parent who makes every effort to accept his would-be son-in-law until his solicitor proves that the man is actually a criminal. James, by coincidence or not, has combined the situations to achieve the highest dramatic effect by positing a father who is just as emotionally in the wrong as he is intellectually in the right. Dr. Sloper does not love his daughter, which makes the interest that he takes in her dilemma far more damaging

James as drawn by Beerbohm in 1898

than the indifference of Grandet. Catherine provides a *show* which her father watches with cynical amusement, making private bets whether she will "stick" to her suitor or do as she is told. The girl never fully recovers from the double blow to her heart and pride that her lover and father inflict. Between them, they destroy her life. But it takes both — that is the point. In Balzac and Trollope the lover alone is the villain.

The chief beauty of *Washington Square*, as of *Eugénie Grandet*, lies in its expression — by background, characterization, and dialogue — of its mild heroine's mood of long-suffering patience. Everything is ordered, polite, still: the charming old square in the pre-brownstone city, the small, innocent, decorous social gatherings, the formal good manners, the quaint reasonableness of the dialogues. James allows his own nostalgia for the lost city of his childhood to assist him in the famous evocation of the Square:

It was here, as you might have been informed on good authority, that you had come into a world which appeared to offer a variety of sources of interest; it was here that your grandmother lived, in venerable solitude, and dispensed a hospitality which commended itself alike to the infant imaginations and the infant palate; it was here that you took your first walks abroad, following the nursery-maid with unequal step, and sniffing up the strange odour of the ailanthus-trees which at that time formed the principal umbrage of the Square, and diffused an aroma that you were not yet critical enough to dislike as it deserved; it was here, finally, that your first school, kept by a broad-bosomed, broad-based old lady with a ferrule, who was always having tea in a blue cup, with a saucer that didn't match, enlarged the circle both of your observations and your sensations. It was here, at any rate, that my heroine spent many years of her life; which is my excuse for this topographical parenthesis.

Can one conceive of the author of *The Wings of the Dove* supplementing the guilt-ridden Densher's impressions of autumnal Venice with his own memories of visits to the Palazzo Barbaro? Yet the quoted passage helps significantly to establish the mood that is maintained to the end of the novel.

The fact that Catherine Sloper never rises to a great passion but simply encases her broken heart in the outward form of a cheerful, benevolent, charitable old maid seems almost to reflect the unexpressed opinion of her creator that in that simpler time and place there were no great passions, that violent emotions belonged to a wicked old Europe where they necessarily coexisted with the richer art and deeper soul of ancient communities. The pale little drama of Catherine Sloper's unhappy love seems to belong with James's conception of the "thin air" of the New World that he had found an insufficient ambience for his muse. But *Washington Square* is still the finest expression of the point of view informed by that disdain. We need not get irritated unless we grope too deeply behind the artistic intent.

The elements that James introduces to his plot to ripple the placid surface of life on the Square are perfectly in tone with the general mood. Violent ambition, towering passion, murderous revenge — such things would be too much. The villain of *Washington Square* need not be sinister or dangerous, but simply a mildly worthless, thoroughly lazy, gently despicable character who, although related to a "good family," is still not quite a gentleman. For we are made to feel from the beginning that Morris Townsend never really belongs to the society of Washington Square. He looks, at first glance, as if he did, but at a second he is a bit too handsome, a bit too soft, a bit too glib. And then he is mercenary and poor in a world where it is only permissible to be mercenary and rich. Dr. Sloper, Catherine's father, has been rather surprised, actually, at how few fortune hunters seem to besiege the heiresses of New York. In a closed society, where everyone knows everyone, they stick out like jewelry thieves in black masks.

The doctor, of course, has sized up Morris Townsend at once, but then so has everyone else except poor Catherine and her idiotic aunt-companion. The real function of Sloper's sharp intelligence in the book is not to uncover so palpable a fraud as the young man's professed love but to analyze his daughter and draw up estimates of the likelihood of her "sticking" to Townsend or of her giving him up. His way of playing with the unfortunate girl is even more cruel than Townsend's and certainly more destructive of her ultimate happiness. The two snakes in Catherine's garden are really one: her lover's and her father's contempt. Under the gentle bloom of that subdued society the soil is arid. Catherine learns in time to live without love, but her life is a poor enough thing without it.

It is she, however, who prevails in the end over her father. Dr. Sloper's fate is harder than his daughter's. Because he is intelligent in an emotional void — without any real love or sympathy for his fellowmen — he has nothing but intelligence with which to answer his own doubts, and this intelligence betrays him ultimately to absurd conclusions. He loses all sight of the real Catherine in his obsession with what she may be thinking about Townsend, and comes eventually to believe that she has a secret understanding with her absent lover. When she refuses to promise him that she will not marry Townsend after his death, the doctor loses his head entirely and writes a ludicrous codicil to his will, publicly excoriating his placid, middle-aged virgin daughter as a person who persists in regarding "unscrupulous adventurers" as an "interesting class." It is he, not Catherine, who in the end is made a fool. The quiet, ordered life of the Square closes over and survives mere cleverness as it does mere greed.

When *Washington Square* was successfully dramatized into *The Heiress* by Ruth and Augustus Goetz, an interesting alteration was made in the character of Catherine. Emotional frustration is seen as turning her into a moral monster who makes it bitingly clear to her dying father that she has no scrap of affection left for him and who evens her score with broke, beaten, middle-aged Morris Townsend by pretending that she will go off with him and then exulting while he pounds in vain on her locked door. The Goetzes may well have been describing what *would* have been going on in the subconscious mind of James's heroine. It is difficult, in our era, to accept Catherine's placidity as the expression of everything that seethed — or failed to seethe — within her. But it is also possible that human beings may vary even in seeming essentials in different cultures. James's Catherine may be a true picture of such an old maid in Washington Square in the middle of the last century:

From her own point of view the great facts of her career were that Morris Townsend had trifled with her affection, and that her father had broken its spring. Nothing could ever alter these facts; they were always there, like her name, her age, her plain face. Nothing could ever undo the wrong or cure the pain that Morris had inflicted on her, and nothing could ever make her feel towards her father as she felt in her younger years. There was something dead in her life, and her duty was to try and fill the void. Catherine recognized this duty to the utmost; she had a great disapproval of brooding and moping.

In the end, as in the beginning, Catherine accepts everything: her humiliation, her loss, even her recovery.

I had taken for granted that my habit of mentally bracketing *Washington Square* with "The Aspern Papers," which James wrote eight years later, was quite arbitrary until I discovered that the inspiration for both tales was not only similar but noticeably different — so far as one can make out from the notebooks — from that of all the others of his longer works. In each of my bracketed cases the whole plot with all essential details was supplied by an anecdote, whereas in the case of the other fictions the inspiring idea was only a fragment of the finished work. *Washington Square*, as already indicated, was the true story of Fanny Kemble's brother, and "The Aspern Papers" is the disguised account (transferred from Florence to Venice) of Captain Silsbee's violent efforts to obtain papers relating to Shelley and Byron from the ancient Claire Claremont, sole survivor of their romantic circle. Both stories appealed in all their truth to James's sense of the dramatic. He had his scenarios, so to speak, handed to him.

But there is also a similarity of mood and tempo in the two tales. In each a sinister stranger intrudes on quiet lives. The shabby old palazzo in "The Aspern Papers" where Miss Bordereau and her niece live in isolation from the world is even quieter than Dr. Sloper's house on Washington Square. The old woman is almost dead, and her niece is a poor, vapid creature whose only flight of imagination is to make a clumsy effort to use her aunt's private papers as a dot to induce the narrator to marry her. The latter, an incorrigible snoop, a sort of literary Morris Townsend, if Townsend can be imagined with a passion, a would-be biographer who richly deserves the epithet "publishing scoundrel" which Miss Bordereau finally flings at him, shamelessly uses every shabby trick he can think up to gain access to documents that his landlady manifestly does not wish him to see. Yet, unlike the characters in *Washington Square*, those in "The Aspern Papers" live in the eye of a storm. Around them, geographically, is the romantic riot of Venetian colors and behind them, historically, is the romantic glory of the poet, Jeffrey Aspern, and a heroic past where great passions were still possible. Miss Bordereau, an incomparable and magnificent old witch, has survived her whole generation to give to the little people of a smaller world a taste of what they have lost.

The lyrical style of this tale is the finest of the Balzac period. James was the poet of cities: New York in *Washington Square*; Venice in "The Aspern Papers"; Paris in *The Ambassadors*; Boston in *The Bostonians*. A part of his success may be traced to the contrast of the silence of his interiors to the hubbub without. The peace of Madame de Vionnet's parlor in the Faubourg Saint-Germain is found in Olive Chancellor's drawing room overlooking the Charles and again in Miss Bordereau's *piano nobile* and in Dr. Sloper's front parlor. The soul of a great city may be silent.

The International Situation:
The Portrait of a Lady

It has always seemed curious to me that one of the most discussed aspects of James's fiction should be the "international situation." I have never seen what there was to be said about his treatment of this theme after one has noted that his American characters are high-minded and naive and are taken advantage of by their more worldly European acquaintants. James's American girls abroad, his Daisy Millers and Francie Dossons, may be charming creatures, but I do not even think that he deserves the whole credit for introducing them into literature. Caroline Spalding in Anthony Trollope's *He Knew He Was Right* made her appearance long before Bessie Alden in "An Internationl Episode," and she anticipates all of the latter's principal characteristics.

It also seems to me that James is playing a private game in some of these stories. He had had his share of snubs in Victorian society (which must have cultivated arrogance to a degree almost inconceivable to us), and he enjoyed paying back the nobility by having his Yankee heroines turn

down their sons and heirs. Bessie Alden rejects the heir to
a dukedom, and Isabel Archer in *The Portrait of a Lady*
declines the honor of becoming Lady Warburton. When
"An International Episode" first appeared James was candidly delighted with the way British readers resented Bessie Alden's democratic assumptions. Yet he was never one
to overdefy his chosen countrymen, and he sounded a
cautious note in a letter to his mother: "It seems to me
myself that I have been very delicate; but I shall keep off
dangerous ground in future. It is an entirely new sensa-
tion for them (the people here) to be (at all delicately)
ironized or satirized, from the American point of view . . ."

To my thinking the comparison of American with
European values brought out the most superficial side of
James. All his life he was to harp on the "tone of time," the
great European cultural advantage, yet in most of his instances this "time" does not take one back much earlier
than the eighteenth century, which had, after all, its
American counterpart. The culture in which James en-
cased himself, literary, artistic, and even architectural, was
usually not more ancient than that. Another element that
he emphasized was the "thinness" of the American air as
contrasted to the richness of the European. One presumes
that he was referring to the cultural atmosphere — although there are instances where he appears to be actually
speaking of the air he breathes — and certainly it is true
that the American field of letters and arts was bleak compared to that of England and France at the time of his
initial expatriation, but he clouds his distinctions by con-
tinually confusing "culture" with the picturesque ways in
which the British upper class amused itself. Somehow
hunting and riding and weekending and dinner partying
seemed to strike James as parts of the cultural scene. The

fact that he had a sharp eye for the shoddy in the English aristocracy did not keep him from losing his head over the beauty of the right kind of peer with the right kind of tradition in the right kind of castle. There are moments when his vision of England seems as bland as a travel poster.

Now, of course, in his own life (as opposed to that of his characters) he did not live exclusively in the social world. When he went to Paris and London he cultivated the literary figures of the day. In Paris, as a young man, he made the acquaintance of Zola, Daudet, Maupassant, Bourget, and Flaubert. In London he met George Eliot and Tennyson. Over a long life I estimate that he knew, with some degree of intimacy, more eminent men and women of letters, from Thackeray to Ezra Pound, than any other writer in literary history. The literary world provided a continual and necessary balance to the millionaires and the peerage. But this balance is not provided for the characters in the early international tales. As a result they seem constantly absorbed in petty activities.

The baroness in *The Europeans* is bothered by the fact that there are not more servants in the entrance halls of American hotels. She tries to make herself at home in a Boston suburb by spreading shawls over the furniture. Daisy Miller causes a scandal in Rome by a nocturnal visit to the Colosseum with an Italian escort, unchaperoned. Isabel Archer is reproved by her aunt for wanting to sit up at night in the drawing room with two gentlemen, of whom one is her own first cousin, after her hostess has retired. And when characters of different nationalities converse it is almost always about the tighter line of class distinctions drawn to the east of the Atlantic.

I do not question the accuracy of these observations about rules of conduct. I question their importance. For

"The Old Diner-Out. A Memory" (Beerbohm, 1926)

people in society do not live by their own social principles unless it suits them. They show little consistency. If there is a reason for liking Daisy Miller, they will pooh-pooh her walks in the Colosseum or look the other way. If there is a reason for disliking her, they will cut her dead. Proust understood this as no other novelist has ever understood it. James came in time to be vaguely aware of it, but he never liked it. He considered that manners had deteriorated, and he saw this deterioration as symptomatic of a general cultural decline. In manners and morals, he was always a tremendous conservative.

But James usually knew what was wrong with his work. When he sensed triviality in a theme, he put his foot down hard on the moral pedal. To complicate the oversimplicity of these bright, sparkling, but superficial tales, he introduced stern ethical judgments. The American ingenue is seen as not merely more democratic and freer than the Europeans whom she encounters; she is purer and more honest. If she is headstrong, naive, abrupt, even blunt, she is also shiningly, incontrovertibly good. If she is made unhappy, or even done to death, by a cynical, dirty-minded old Europe, it is a tragedy. Good against evil, the brave New World against the wicked Old, such is the melodramatic international conflict as James conceived it. "Madame de Mauves" is the earliest example of this. The American heroine's only fault is that she is naively romantic; her French husband's only virtue is that he ultimately commits suicide after perversely and belatedly falling in love with her.

My trouble is that I do not believe in any of it, and I wonder if James really did. I suppose that there were Daisy Millers in Rome in his day, but I doubt that any of them died of snubs. James was soon enough to see his rich compatriots as predators, prowling about a crumbling Europe and bearing off masterpieces. He thought that the situation had changed. Maybe it was simply that his angle of vision had improved. But the redeeming thing about his overconcern with the "international situation" was that it produced *The Portrait of a Lady*. The explanation of the paradox that so deep a work of fiction should spring from so shallow a subject is that the subject provides the novel with no more than its starting point. James went on to ponder questions which had a good deal to do with his characters being American but much less to do with their being international. Isabel Archer's tragedy might almost have been acted out in New York.

We can see a forecast of this in "Daisy Miller." All the ladies who condemn Daisy for going about Rome un-chaperoned with Mr. Giovanelli are Americans. Perhaps an uneasy sense of social inferiority to Italian noble families makes them more censorious of a nonconforming countrywoman than they would have been at home, but one imagines that they did their share of staring from carriages on Fifth Avenue as well as on the Corso. Daisy Miller might have been snubbed in a drawing room on Gramercy Park and died of a cold caught in the Rambles. The essence of the story lies more in her innocent naiveté than in her exposure to Europe. The drama of the story lies in the opposition of Americans to Americans, not Americans to Europeans. Daisy is a goose, however charming a one, not to recognize that there are people — of *every* nationality — who believe that flirtation implies sexual intercourse. We certainly believe it today.

James stacked the cards against Daisy. Would Mrs. Walker *really* have turned her back on the poor girl at her own party? What saves the story is that James realizes that he has stacked the cards, and out of the adjustment required by this realization springs the unique quality of the piece. What Daisy dies of is not the disapproval of society, about which she cares not a hoot, but the disapproval of the priggish Winterbourne, whom she loves. Everything depends on Daisy's death. In a longer work the coincidence of her fatal fever coming at the same time as her disappointed passion would not be acceptable. For had Daisy recovered from her fever, she would easily have overcome Winterbourne's reservations, and there would have been a happy ending. This would have been banal, as can be seen in the dull little play into which James converted his charming story. "Daisy Miller" depends utterly on its brief, vivid snapshots of Daisy and the pathetic climax of her extinction.

Although all the action of *The Portrait of a Lady* (except for a brief chapter in Albany) takes place in England, France, and Italy, the characters, except for Lord Warburton, are all Americans. Isabel Archer, Caspar Goodwood, and Henrietta Stackpole are Americans of origin and upbringing who are having their first adult European experience as the novel commences. Mr. and Mrs. Touchett are Americans who have lived in Europe all their adult lives but who have been reared at home and have preserved their essential American characteristics. Ralph Touchett, their son, has lived all his life in England, but has kept in touch with his native land. He is the one true cosmopolitan of the novel. Edward Rosier, Madame Merle, Gilbert Osmond, and the Countess Gemini, on the other hand, are Americans who have ceased to think of America or to take the smallest interest in their birthplace. They have been Europeanized without ever entirely belonging to Europe. What James has done by setting these characters against a backdrop of London, Florence, and Rome is to put different facets of the American character into higher relief than he could have done with an American situs. From a strictly artistic point of view I have always regretted the British nationality of Lord Warburton. Impenitently, I see him as a younger American banking partner of Mr. Touchett.

Isabel is, of course, the victim of a plot. The clever Madame Merle induces her indolent and selfish ex-lover, Gilbert Osmond, to court her so that he may obtain her fortune and endow Pansy, the bastard daughter of Osmond and Madame Merle. And Isabel's fortune, which so proves her undoing, is the result of another, if kinder plot. Ralph Touchett has induced his father to leave it to Isabel because, as a beneficent but too curious invalid, he wants to see what she will do with "a little wind in her sails." So one might say that Isabel is the victim of a double conspiracy: one, an old-fashioned mercenary scheme of the European sort and the other, a naive but perverse American form of pastime. But the person who really ties the cords of Isabel's fate is Isabel herself. And this is the essence of the novel.

She is the loveliest and most appealing of all James's heroines. She is very fine, very straight, totally honest, and candid to a fault, and she has a charm which captivates every other character as well as the reader. Isabel has a high sense that she must be prepared for her destiny — whatever that destiny may be. She has no great opinion of her own capacities, but she appreciates that she is not made of common materials. She apprehends that she may be reserved for something, if not necessarily illustrious, at least rather fine. She does not for a minute assume that it will be happy. Indeed a certain anticipation of her doom appears to hang about her from the beginning. It is this which gives her her especially American flavor.

Success crowds in on her, jostles her. Her rich aunt, Mrs. Touchett, swoops down to take her off to Europe. Caspar Goodwood, a brave young textile manufacturer, follows her with passionate proposals of marriage. Her cousin Ralph devotes all his waking thoughts to her. Lord Warburton offers to make her his viscountess. Her uncle bequeaths her a fortune. Remarkably, James makes Isabel's success quite credible; she seems to offer to each new acquaintance precisely what he or she most needs. But Isabel does not care for easy successes. They seem crude, perhaps obvious to her. She has a kind of hubris about the gifts of the gods. The smashing forcefulness of Caspar Goodwood, the high social position of Lord Warburton, the glitter of her own inherited wealth — these things make her uneasy. She cannot believe that her fate is so simple. She tells Lord Warburton that she would be trying to escape it if she marries him. "I can't escape unhappiness," she declares. She confesses to her cousin Ralph that Warburton is too perfect and that his perfection would irritate her.

She must give as well as take, then, in the strange romantic destiny that she dimly descries. Of course, it need not be a "successful" fate, by simple American or English standards. And when Madame Merle guides her to Gilbert Osmond, poor Isabel sees in his love of art and beauty, in his seeming scorn of the world, in his very idleness, the independence of a great mind which has cast aside the trappings of the workaday existence of busy American industrialists and of politically minded British peers. Osmond, surrounded by his perfect pictures and bibelots on the top of his hill beside Florence, makes even the best natured of her good-natured friends seem shallow. "He was like a sceptical voyager strolling on the beach while he waited for the tide, looking seaward yet not putting to sea. It was in all this that she had found her occasion. She would launch his boat for him; she would be his providence; it would be a good thing to love him."

I know of no finer passages in all of James than those where he uncovers the true character of Osmond and the terrible disillusionment of Isabel. The fact that he has already indicated the wrongness of her choice, not only through direct glimpses of Osmond but through the unanimous adverse opinion of all Isabel's friends, somehow does not make her horror on encountering the "mansion" of her husband's mental habitation an anticlimax: "It was the house of darkness, the house of dumbness, the house of suffocation. Osmond's beautiful mind gave it neither light nor air; Osmond's beautiful mind indeed seemed to peep down from a small high window and mock her."

And what of the vulgar world from which Osmond had seemed so carefully to remove himself, from which they were to live unspotted? This base, ignoble world, it appears, "was after all what one was to live for; one was to keep it for ever in one's eye, in order not to enlighten or convert or redeem it, but to extract from it some recognition of one's own superiority." Everything that Osmond does is pose. "His life on his hilltop at Florence had been the conscious attitude of years. His solitude, his *ennui*, his love for his daughter, his good manners, his bad manners, were so many features of a mental image constantly present to him as a model of impertinence and mystification."

Isabel's acceptance of her fate is explained in the title. She sees the deceit and the entrapment, but she also sees that she has made a choice. "When a woman has made such a mistake, there was only one way to repair it — to accept it." Her friends think that she must fear her sinister husband, but the wonderful thing about Isabel is that she is not in the least afraid of him. She is afraid only of the ugliness of a public rupture of her marriage, of demonstrating her private failure to the world. However misguided this may seem to our century — and indeed it seemed so to many readers in the last — one cannot deny that Isabel's sticking to her wretched home and to her wretched stepdaughter shows a certain high style. Nor is she in the least subservient to Osmond. She crosses his wishes whenever she deems it right to do so, as when she interferes between his daughter Pansy and Lord Warburton and when she goes to Ralph's deathbed in England. She is always perfectly direct and honest with Osmond. But she has agreed to be his wife before the world, and this she will be while she has breath in her body. For better or worse. That was to be a lady in her time.

Isabel's pathetic plight, as I have said, is American in its particular combination of romantic idealism with a willingness to suffer, even an expectation of suffering. She is a dupe, but such a lovely one and such a splendidly good sport, so square in admitting her own folly, that her being "put in a cage," as her cousin expresses it, is even more heartbreaking than if she had not made love to her destiny. But the evil that confronts her, the evil that captures her — is it European? Madame Merle wishes to convert Isabel's fortune into a dower for her daughter, and Osmond wishes to use this same money to build the lavish setting for his ultimate pose. But might such a pair not have operated in New York? Nineteenth-century Manhattan had more than its share of such adventurers. There is, of course, a suaveness and a style about the conspirators that seems more European than Yankee, but I suggest that Madame Merle and Osmond represent integral parts of the American psyche.

The most important reason, to my mind, for setting the novel in Europe is simply that the visual background provides the same rich charge to Isabel's imagination that it did to James's own. The drama of an American girl with the world at her feet was more exciting in the 1870s if that world was the glittering Old World rather than the still raw New. Furthermore, it is difficult to see how a dilettante in New York could have captured Isabel's fancy in quite the same way as could a dilettante living in Florence. One does not immediately see Osmond in a small flat on Washington Square filled with bibelots, taking Isabel on a guided tour through the still exiguous collection at the newly founded Metropolitan Museum of Art. No, it is better to see him in his hilltop abode with a beautiful Florence, which he thoroughly understands, at his feet.

When I say that the *Portrait of a Lady* is not, properly speaking, an international novel, I mean that the contrast of manners and mores no longer has the importance that it had in the earlier stories. Isabel adapts herself to European standards with almost no trouble at all. She has one brief scene, already cited, with her aunt about sitting up in the drawing room with two gentlemen after Mrs. Touchett has retired, but unlike Daisy Miller she wisely gives in to her aunt. She knows that these small conventions make little difference. To defy them is to make too much of them. James in 1881 had come to recognize that transatlantic distinctions were slight enough to be left to the minor characters. Henrietta Stackpole who insists on them in every paragraph where she appears is a ridiculous character, almost a caricature. James's sense of her importance is summed up in the scene where she asks Lord Warburton if the silver cross which his sister is wearing is a badge of rank. He tells her, straight-faced, that it is a decoration always worn by the eldest daughters of viscounts.

After the *Portrait of a Lady* James continued, almost out of habit, as it were, with his international romances. But he was constrained more and more to make them matters of comedy. In "Pandora" the foreign observer in Washington who cannot make out the different gradations of the American social positions is an absurd German count whom the reader is not expected to take seriously. In "The Siege of London" Mrs. Headway, who batters her way into London society to marry a peer, is hardly a credible character. She comes from the West and has been married so many times that nobody can count the number of her husbands. James can hardly have expected his reader to accept for true the proposition that Lord Demesne's family would permit such an alliance without checking the woman's antecedents in some way more thorough than merely querying one man who has known her.

"Lady Barbarina," unlike the last two mentioned tales, is thoroughly serious, but it is not a real-life situation. It is a hypothesis. James has set himself the exercise of reversing the usual international title purchase. Instead of an American heiress buying a marquess, he would invent an American heir buying a marquess's daughter. Christopher Newman in *The American* had tried and failed, but James had become convinced that in that book he had exaggerated the pride of the Bellegardes and their reluctance to "cash in." He would try again.

Apparently, up to 1888, no daughter of a great English peer *had* married an American. The two English noble-

women whom James sends to New York are sisters: Lady
Barbarina, the elder, becomes the wife of a rich American
doctor, Jackson Lemon (why *that* name?), and Lady
Agatha goes to America to keep her company. One certainly cannot deny the verisimilitude of their types. "Lady
Barb" is the stolid, unmovable, unimpressed, stubborn,
utterly British female aristocrat who sulks when removed
from the country house and hunting field and refuses to
admit the very existence of any values but her own. There
were plenty of her type in the nineteenth century. There
are even a few left today. And Lady Agatha is equally
credible as her opposite, the reckless, feckless, breathless
English noblewoman who adores everything that is wildest
and wooliest in the American West and elopes with an
adventurer she believes to be a sort of cowboy. But the
story has the ennui attached to an impossible task. There is
nothing under the sun that Jackson Lemon can do to make
his dull wife like New York, and one feels that he should
have seen this himself from the beginning. It is a kind of
cautionary tale to warn American millionaires away from
the London matrimonial market. But is it fair? Jackson
Lemon might have made a success of a marriage to Lady
Agatha. Only a nincompoop would have married her sister.

Finally, as a kind of *envoi* to the international romance,
there is the beautiful little novella *The Reverberator* in which
James returned to his happiest method of dealing with this
subject. As with "Daisy Miller" and *The Portrait of a Lady* he
concentrated on Americans in Europe meeting other
Americans in Europe, the difference between them consisting essentially (but by no means entirely) in the length
of their exposure to "abroad." In *The Reverberator* Mr. Dosson and his two daughters, Delia and Francie, are Ameri-

can to the core. With respect to the father, at least, it is too late for the European experience to find the smallest fissure through which to enter his being. The Proberts, on the other hand, have lived in France so long that they have become totally Gallicized. The three daughters have all married French nobles, and the father, like Mr. Dosson, is beyond the possibility of any new national conversion. The love of Francie and Gaston is the only possible link between the two families, and it is a highly precarious one. When Francie exposes the Proberts' darkest secrets to her newspaper reporter friend, Mr. Flack, the breach is quick and final. Gaston must break with his family to marry her. Happily, he does not hesitate.

What gives to the tale its peculiar tensity is the heightened animosity of civil conflict. If the Proberts had been really French, they might have forgiven Francie her American indiscretion. And if they had not been American, Francie and her father and sister would not have so bitterly resented the Proberts' indignation and snobbishness. The crunch of the situation is a class crunch, rather than an international one. The Proberts look down on the Dossons, way down, and the Dossons would like to know who the hell the Proberts think they are. It is an American situation with American resentments, and Paris, where, as Oscar Wilde said, good Americans go when they die, is peculiarly the right setting for it.

The Social Novels:
The Princess Casamassima
and *The Bostonians*

In one year, 1886, James published two of his longest and most considerable novels, *The Princess Casamassima* and *The Bostonians*, representing the climax of his intense and prolonged dedication to the task of becoming the Balzac of his generation. For the first time he broadened the scope of his representations to take in the working classes, and in the earlier of these chronicles he addressed his attention to no less a subject than a radical international conspiracy to subvert the foundations of the European social order.

The Princess Casamassima is the finest example of James's astonishing virtuosity. It is done, to put it crudely, with spit and sealing wax. James had only the most superficial interest in the international socialist movement and little more than a child's sense of the picturesque aspects of the London poor. It is true that he roamed the slums of the city in preparation for the novel and even visited a prison, but he had no real sympathy or identification with the lower orders, and his description of a meeting of socialist

71

workers at a public house called the "Sun and Moon" has some of the heavily massed "local color" of an elaborate Henry Irving stage set. The poor are shown as largely obsessed with the social doings of the rich, and the menacing revolution is conceived in terms of an operatic 1789. Yet most of the major characters, oddly enough, are aristocrats: the hero, Hyacinth Robinson, is the bastard of a peer's son; the Princess Casamassima is the estranged wife of a rich Roman of ancient lineage; Madame Grandoni and Lady Aurora are noble. But at least they are real, very real. The lower-class characters seem to be the products of the author's close emulation of Dickens (the visit to the prison reads like a chapter from *Oliver Twist*), and one of them, Rose Muniment, has an actual counterpart in *Our Mutual Friend*. Only Paul, her brother, and Millicent Henning, the cockney salesgirl, strike me as originals of James's own imagination.

And what of the social message? It appears to be contained in the sad parable of Hyacinth. Brought up by the old-maid dressmaker to whom his French mother has consigned him after her conviction for murdering his noble sire, he daydreams of the greater world from which he has sprung and fancies revenge through revolution. James solves the problem of his trade by making him a bookbinder so that he can be exposed to literature at least through its covers. Somehow, Hyacinth manages to educate himself and to develop into a Jamesian hero. Rarely has such a flower bloomed in less likely soil. He even picks up French and Italian and becomes such a natural "swell" that he is pressed into service by a radical group who need him to assassinate a duke at a great party where he must mingle with the guests. But Hyacinth then meets the Princess Casamassima, a world-weary refugee from aristocratic so-

ciety who wants the final jag of communism, and falls under
her spell — or at least under the spell of her elegant possessions and style of living. Haunted by the idea that his
revolution will destroy the outward beauty that he has belatedly discovered in upper-class lives and reduce the
world to a crude uniformity, Hyacinth commits suicide
rather than carry out his oath to the radicals. His final vote
is for the china shop and not the bull.

The naiveté of James as a social thinker has always been
somewhat embarrassing to his devotees, but I think it is
better to face it than to slough it over. I have observed a
tendency in critics either to endorse James *in toto* or to
throw him out. But there is no need for such extremes.
There is a much greater chance, in my opinion, for the
ultimate survival of James's greater works if we clearly
mark out the areas where he has shown himself a bit of an
ass. His passion for the social order of the English countryside, for great houses and bric-a-brac, for the minutiae
of parlor manners and parlor distinctions — and the utter,
unsmiling seriousness with which he takes it all — offer
some justification for Theodore Roosevelt's angry remark
that James's "snobbish little tales" about upper-class life in
Europe made him ashamed that their author "had once
been" an American. If all this is out in the open, it is much
less troublesome. One can then put it in perspective
against the great things.

And now let us take a look at what James accomplished in
this novel with the paucity of his material. It is simple wiz-
ardry. He is like a great repertory actor who can play Justice
Shallow as well as King Lear. One may wish that he would
stick to Lear and still appreciate the comic role. For *The
Princess Casamassima*, with a theme which it is impossible to
take seriously and a background worthy of comic opera, is

nonetheless a warm and absorbing novel. The plucky little bookbinder, with his romantic conscience and noble air and his fatal susceptibility to beautiful things, is an appealing hero, and we follow the unhappy story of his divided loyalties with unremitting interest and sympathy. It is a most lively tale. If James has not been quite sure what to do with the whole, he makes up for it by polishing the parts. They must stand or fall by themselves.

The Princess Casamassima herself — what are we meant to deduce from her character and curious situation? We have already met her as Christina Light in *Roderick Hudson*. She is magnificent and beautiful, both in mind and body, but she has no heart for her fellow humans. She passes from one fad to another, from one man to another. She drops Captain Sholto for Hyacinth, Hyacinth for Paul Muniment. Are we meant to feel that she has got her proper comeuppance when Paul turns on her, after the last of her money is gone, and tells her to go back to her husband? I am not sure. And when Madame Grandoni points out that the princess has not really stripped herself of all worldly goods, but that she has put some of her best things in storage and keeps a maid concealed upstairs, are we meant to take this as showing that the princess is basically superficial and self-deceiving? Again, I am not sure.

I suspect that James never quite made up his own mind about his heroine. She is very much alive, so much so that I wonder if she did not begin to exasperate her creator as she does his readers. Her cool arrogance, her amazing composure, her bland assumption that everyone will do exactly what she wants — even when balanced against her fairness, her knowledge of herself and of how she must strike other people — make of her ultimate defeat an experience that rather pleases at least this reader. Has she been raised up only to be knocked down? Perhaps James himself quailed before the picture that his finale seems to make inevitable: that of his proud heroine reduced to poverty and forced to eat humble pie before her triumphant husband. It is difficult to imagine her doing so, but it is equally difficult to see her coping with indigence. She will not add up. It was better to drop the curtain when James dropped it. After all, the princess is a fairy story character, not like Millicent Henning, Hyacinth's cockney friend who, although conceived along the simplest lines (she is always tossing her head at the pretensions of others to be above her), is a thoroughly successful characterization of a member of her class.

The most interesting male character in the book, after the hero, is Paul Muniment, who is responsible for Hyacinth's fatal assignment. Paul is James's only serious contribution to the discussion of socialism in the novel. In this robust, unsusceptible, stony-hearted man we have a faint glimmer of a true revolutionist. Paul is never excited; he despises drama and eloquence; he has no use for love or hate. He is always practical, always realistic. He will not sacrifice Hyacinth unless it is necessary for the cause, but when it becomes necessary, he will do so with a shrug. Like a true Marxist he has no rancor against the "haves" of the world, but when the time comes, he will use his gun on them as a farmer might use an insecticide. I think that James endows him with too much good breeding when he makes him blush at the princess's accusation that he has been after her money, but it is a rare false note, like his sentimental attachment for the crippled sister who came out of Dickens.

If *The Princess Casamassima* is a work of fancy, *The Bostonians* is one of sober fact. James in later years downgraded this remarkable novel. He found it loose and prolix, and he omitted it from the New York Edition of his fiction. Certainly it is too long, and the characters, toward the end, tend to repeat themselves monotonously and yet inadequately on the meager number of aspects of the women's suffrage movement about which their creator had bothered to "bone up." But I suspect that in 1886 James must have known that he had written, if not a great sociological document, at least a great psychological drama. And I doubt that he considered Basil Ransom, his unreconstructed Mississippian, as hollow a hero as he later professed to regard him. I think he knew at the time that what he had created was a man, a real man.

Also in later years, as shown in the profound chapter on Richmond in *The American Scene*, James came to recognize how little the South had learned from the Civil War. He was to make some very penetrating comments on its treatment of blacks, and this may have changed his opinion of what a man like Ransom really was like. But in the 1870s and 1880s the South was invested with the glamor of a lost cause. As the northern states seemed to darken under the dirty cloud of industrial prosperity and political corruption, the stricken, humiliated South took on a purged, heroic look. It is no coincidence that there is a resemblance between the heroes of *The Bostonians* and *Democracy*, both former Confederate officers. Henry James and Henry Adams each drew material from the personality of a Mississippi senator, Lucius G. C. Lamar, who, unlike them, had fought through the war.

Both writers were acutely conscious of not having served in the army. James always waxed emotional about those who had served and died. In his memoirs and in *The American Scene* he became even lyrical about their sacrifice. Obviously, he must have felt guilt at having lived and prospered at their expense. As time went on, the warriors on both sides tended to fuse in his mind. They joined to become symbols of a lost virility. Basil Ransom, visiting a war memorial in Cambridge, forgets the whole question of sides and parties: "The simple emotion of the old fighting-time came back to him, and the monument around him seemed an embodiment of that memory." In Ransom's long, brown, hard leanness, in his scorn of the tinselly second-rate, in his pride and aloofness, and in his susceptibility to pretty girls, I seem also to make out a suggestion of Captain Oliver Wendell Holmes, Jr., who occupied more of the attention of Minny Temple in the first year after the war than did her cousin Harry James.

I do not think it too fanciful to speculate that James's later low opinion of Ransom may have something to do with the mild embarrassment that writers feel about characters conceived in earlier periods of intense emotional identification. Ransom is a character conceived in opposites to James: he is a provincial, a warrior, a womanizer. He likes law and politics; he dislikes social affairs. He is the perfect spokesman for James's detestation of the meretricious and phony in American humanitarian movements, of the charlatanism, hypocrisy, and sanctimoniousness of the Boston Yankee on the platform. What might be taken ill from James, the expatriate, bookish observer, comes better from Ransom, the soldier who has risked his life daily for four years on the battlefields and who is therefore more entitled to sneer at public shriekers. When James speaks of Ransom in the following passage, I have little doubt that he is setting forth his own convictions: "I suppose he was very conceited, for he was much addicted to judging his age. He thought it talkative, querulous, hysterical, maudlin, full of false ideas, of unhealthy germs, of extravagant, dissipated habits, for which a great reckoning was in store. He was an immense admirer of the late Thomas Carlyle, and was very suspicious of the encroachments of modern democracy."

We see then that Basil Ransom has been invented to combat all that James found wrong with the America he had quit in the 1870s for Europe. But how was Ransom to "get at" his era? James could not very well have him take on the whole nation in another civil war. He did not want to call his book *The Americans*. He had therefore to reduce Ransom's antagonist to workable dimensions, and he seemed to find what he needed in the turbid eddy of false philanthropy that centered in the city of Boston. Boston also offered him what he always needed: a contrast. Behind all the ranting and the raving, behind all the sententiousness and the hypocrisy, there rose, high and grim and silent, the monuments of the heroic age, the age of the great abolitionists, when Boston had led the crusade against slavery. It made for just the right ironic twist that the champion of the old true against the modern phony should be a veteran of the defeated South.

Basil Ransom against Boston, a real man against a city of paper men: here at last was the perfect formula for the great Balzacian novel. But on a closer look what *are* the philanthropies that are so false and vapid? James did not know too much about these; he was simply sure of the particular atmosphere which emanated from a particular part of Boston. But he had to pick a movement, and he picked the one that seemed to require the least homework: that of women's suffrage. What could there be to say about women's suffrage that even a bachelor living in London could not readily imagine? The trouble was caused by the great length of his novel. Long before the halfway point it becomes evident that the author has nothing to say about the wrongs toward women but the most obvious and sentimental things. Basically, he was writing a social novel, with all the necessary crowds and background, but without a real theme.

Even the title is misleading. For who *are* the Bostonians? The Tarrants (who live in Cambridge) are too bizarre and odious to be typical; their daughter Verena is not Bostonian at all; Dr. Prance might exist anywhere; Miss Birdseye, who comes from Connecticut, seems to belong more to the abolitionist movement than to any one place. Olive Chancellor, of course, is Bostonian to the core — unforgettably, inimitably. She is all Beacon Street, all passion, all conscience; she represents her native town like the figure on the prow of an old clipper ship. Perhaps the title of the novel should have been in the singular.

What then grows out of all this chatter about the wrongs suffered by women? Simply a great novel about sex, the only one in the Jamesian canon. The reader feels the attraction between Ransom and Verena as an irresistible physical tug. That may not seem an unusual thing in a novel, but it is in James's. I do not really feel it anywhere else in his work except perhaps between Madame de Vionnet and Chad Newsome in *The Ambassadors*. In all the other novels and tales where sexual attraction is stated, I simply accept it. But in *The Bostonians*, I sense very strongly the passion which shackles two people into a union that neither would for a moment desire without it. Ransom and Verena must copulate. Without the prospect of that act he would vastly prefer his bachelor's life and she her platform career.

The dominant sexuality of Ransom is not posited by James as necessarily a "good" thing. But it is a natural force. Opposed by a group of screaming women, even by a rich and determined lesbian, it mows down all before it. James conceives Verena as a natural woman temporarily perverted by shoddy parents and then more durably estranged from the norm by the forceful nature of Olive Chancellor. Verena loves the malarkey of romanticism, the gushiness of public speaking, the easy tears of distant injustices. She enjoys the illusion of hard work by a cozy fire in Olive's comfortable Charles Street house, snug in the cold Boston winter; she adores the ethereal soaring of their spirits and the gratifying applause of lecture audiences. But when she at last meets a man, a real man, a warrior who has killed other men in combat and who desires her, she is paralyzed. Is it too Freudian to detect phallic imagery produced by James's subconscious in this passage?

When she saw him a little way off, about five o'clock — the hour she usually went out to meet him — waiting for her at a bend of the road which lost itself, after a winding, straggling mile or two, in the indented, insulated "point," where the wandering bee droned through the hot hours with a vague, misguided flight, she felt that his tall, watching figure, with the low horizon behind, represented well the importance, the towering eminence he had in her mind — the fact that he was just now, to her vision, the most definite and upright, the most incomparable, object in the world. If he had not been at his post when she expected him she would have had to stop and lean against something, for weakness; her whole being would have throbbed more painfully than it throbbed at present, though finding him there made her nervous enough. And who was he, what was he? she asked herself.

The stormy scene at the end where Ransom exercises to the full his male dominion and obliges Verena to give up her lecture even while a record audience is filling the Boston Music Hall with its impatient stamping makes a superb dramatic climax. Ransom triumphs, of course, and leads Verena away, her face shrouded from the angry mob, her eyes full of tears which, according to the final sentence, will not be the last that she is destined to shed. I do not think that James meant to imply by this that Verena's marriage would be unhappy. He was merely suggesting that there would be plenty of problems ahead for such a couple. There would have been far more in a life shared with Olive Chancellor.

The sexual drama exploding in the final climax would have made *The Bostonians* a good novel, but Olive Chancellor and Miss Birdseye are what give it its claim to greatness. Surely they rank among James's finest creations. Olive is drawn so vividly that we can make deductions about her that James may not have made: notably that she is a lesbian. The sexual energy that she has subconsciously diverted makes her throb with intensity. She seethes with passions: the passion to do right, the passion to help women, the passion to promote the career of Verena Tarrant, the passion to oppose Basil Ransom. When her emotions finally find an object, as they do in Verena, she becomes a formidable force. In the end it is she alone, not the women's movement at all, who is holding Verena from Ransom. The weak-spirited girl is torn between a fierce man and a fiercer woman. Ransom prevails only because Verena is not a lesbian. I wonder if James's ultimate recognition of the real theme of his novel may not have had something to do with its exclusion from the New York Edition. It may be objected that he could not have failed to recognize anything so obvious. But James could be very naive in certain matters. It was not with farcical intent that he introduced a character called Fanny Assingham into the most lacquered of all his novels.

William James objected to the character of Miss Birdseye as a lampoon of Miss Elizabeth Peabody, the great Boston lady of causes. This was quite in keeping with the older brother's lifelong habit of denigrating the work of the younger, of keeping him "down," a habit that reached its climax in his refusal of membership in the National Academy because Henry had been asked first. No objective relative could have wished to hurt Henry's feelings by criticizing his portrayal of Miss Birdseye, a modern saint. She might be a Giotto. For not only do we sense the heroism, the humility, the dignity of the drab little woman; we note also the dilution of her personality resulting from a kind of leaking goodness, her lack of discrimination, her loss of taste or tang. Miss Birdseye has suppressed her own personality; she has given away all that she has, and James is able to face the possibility that in an age when faith has ebbed the saint may have turned into a cipher. Miss Birdseye is almost a social novel by herself.

The Artist and Writer
in James's Fiction:
The Tragic Muse

Justice Oliver Wendell Holmes, Jr., who knew him well as a young man, wrote: "Henry James never lets up on his high aims. There are not infrequent times when a bottle of wine, a good dinner, a girl of some trivial sort can fill the hour for me." I suspect that James would not have objected to this observation. In later years he inclined to the position that such asceticism was necessary not only for him, but for all creative artists. He became fond of playing the part of the celibate high priest of fiction.

In his many novels and tales about artists I make out three principal temptations for the would-be ascetic: first, the temptation to lower artistic standards for worldly gain; second, the urge to lead a social life at the expense of art; and, finally, love. The first temptation may be dealt with summarily. It does not really exist. Greville Fane in the story bearing her name may write potboilers, but she is incapable of anything better. When a true artist, like Ralph Limbert in "The Next Time," tries to write salable trash, he succeeds only in creating further masterpieces. To James's mind a small talent could never be elevated, and a great one could hardly be prostituted. "The Lesson of the Master," which is generally considered the classic example of this temptation, I prefer to classify under the third category: love.

The second temptation was peculiarly James's own. As a young man he threw himself into the turbid waters of a London social life. Of course, he tried to persuade himself that he was gathering subject material, but anyone who has played the social game knows how quickly one arrives at the point of diminishing returns. After a single week of the London season, an observer as shrewd as James could have easily put together what the balance was bound to be like. One can feel in the very irritation betrayed in his later satires of importunate hostesses the intensity of his attraction to the "great world" and his disgust at his own weakness in letting it waste his time. He came to feel about a weekend bid as a reformed smoker feels about a proffered cigarette.

"The Death of the Lion" is the great story of the second temptation. The poor old novelist Neil Paraday is simply done to death by a weekend hostess and her guests, and his precious manuscript is lost on a train. But it is only a parable; one is not meant to take as true the assassination of the unhappy artist. James is pointing out, with biting laughter, that the social world will never understand the artist or his work, but that it will gobble him up for whatever celebrity value he may have acquired. For a serious writer to expose himself to such a weekend is as foolhardy as for a bleeding man to go swimming in a shark-infested sea. He should content himself with the understanding of the initiated, like the devoted reader of Ralph Limbert in "The Next

Time" who says: "I used to talk about his work, but I seldom talk now: the brotherhood of the faith have become, like the Trappists, a silent order."

The final temptation, love, is the most important, not because it was James's own, but because it wasn't. I see no evidence in the five volumes of Leon Edel's great biography that James ever consciously renounced love for art, or ever had to struggle to do so. Certainly there was no woman in his life. He may have constructed in his fantasy a kind of posthumous romance with his cousin Minny Temple — presumably unilateral, for her letters show no such feeling on her part — but she was conveniently dead, and her loveliness was available for conversion into art. So far as his own sex was concerned, there is no reliable evidence that he ever had a love affair, although it seems clear that he was inclined to sentimental attachments to younger males. If there was any "renunciation," it must have been here, but I doubt that it would have been motivated by any need to keep himself pure for art. I incline to the opinion that like so many of his contemporaries, like so many men, for that matter, in Christian history (up at least to our own day), he was terrified of the moral and social stigma attached to homosexuality. He probably believed that it was wicked, for he always referred to Oscar Wilde with the deepest contempt.

Why then was James so preoccupied with the threat of love to the artist? The theme appears as early as *Roderick Hudson*, where the young sculptor sacrifices his art to his passion for Christina Light. Why, if James himself had not had to give up women for his art, and if he had given up men for quite other reasons, was it so emotionally necessary for him to view the true artist as a kind of monk, totally dedicated to the tending of his altar? He must have known that genius can survive myriad distractions. He was familiar with the crowded lives of Shakespeare, of Balzac, of Wagner. He knew that Thackeray and Dickens had labored to support expensive families. Indeed, he was acutely aware of the case of Flaubert, the one writer whose credo of dedication was as high as his own and who had killed his art in the very fury of his application.

I suggest that James's theory was the fruit of self-dramatization. Any American male of his background and generation would have been bound to suspect that a failure to fight in the Civil War, followed by the failure either to marry or to go into business, impugned his virility. I even go so far as to connect this suspicion with his expatriation. What simpler and more natural inner process could there be for a wounded ego than to dress up a failure of manhood in the robes of a voluntary asceticism, of a dedicated priestliness? James's memoirs were to trace his biography in terms of the development of the observing eye. All that might have otherwise been deemed passive, feminine, evasive, even cowardly, becomes instead the necessary conduct and education of a great artist.

So anxious was James to convince himself of the truth of this image of himself that he destroyed in a bonfire all his private papers and correspondence. Again and again in his fiction his characters express horror at the idea of posthumous revelations, of intrusions into privacy. In the end he wanted to turn his own life into a great novel in the final style, and to some extent he succeeded. Dozens of critics have taken him at his own evaluation. But I have a greater opinion of the strength of James's genius than he himself had. I believe that had he lived in a semidetached villa in Maida Vale with a nagging wife and ten children, he would still have written *The Golden Bowl* and *The Wings of the Dove*. And I doubt that the domestic appendages which I hypothesize would have been any more distracting than his endless fussing over the domestic arrangements of Lamb House.

If James's austere vision of a great writer's removed existence had little to do with actuality, it nonetheless generated one of his finest tales, "The Lesson of the Master." For there it does not matter whether or not we believe that Henry St. George has *really* crippled a major talent by currying popularity to maintain an opulent style of living for the wife and children whom he loved. It is only necessary that St. George should believe it himself and that he should convince Paul Overt that it is so. Actually James's picture of the charming, easygoing, affable, well-dressed gentleman of letters is so vivid, and somehow so total for its type — like a Sargent portrait — that I find myself wondering if such a man could have ever really possessed the "hard, gem-like flame." Isn't it possible that James is hinting that St. George has written as well as he ever could write? That those early novels were overpraised and perhaps essentially like their polished, beautiful, slick successors? And that Paul Overt himself suspects this, particularly when St. George, after urging him to celibacy, walks off with his girl? But such fancies only enhance the fascination of the story. I go so far as to speculate that the fine tone of St. George, his very charm in fact, may be part of the reward of the world for having given up the peak of Parnassus and that Paul Overt, upon attaining that height, may find himself a bit of a curmudgeon.

The issue at stake in "The Lesson of the Master" is dramatically, even fantastically put, and that is perfectly proper for a short story. But when James chose to explore the general problem in depth, as he did in *The Tragic Muse*, the last novel of his Balzac phase, he had to be realistic. In asking his readers to consider, over several hundred pages, all that a young parliamentarian of distinguished political lineage must give up to become a painter, as contrasted with how little a young woman of decayed gentility and near-bohemianism need give up to become an actress, James had to offer a factual setup that could be taken very seriously indeed. If his hero Nick Dormer's problem is to be spread over three volumes, we must be convinced that it is a real one.

The case of a son locked into a family heritage has been a common enough subject in fiction, but I do not know of one more convincingly depicted than that of Nick Dormer. I should imagine that even readers of our time, when tradition counts for so much less, would comprehend his fix. To begin with, his older brother, the heir, Percy, has behaved with total irresponsibility, taking the family property and converting it to his pleasures, while his mother, Lady Agnes, and his sisters, Grace and Biddy, must make do with a pittance. These three ladies depend utterly on Nick to reestablish them in the social world by capturing the political laurels which belonged to his late father and to ease their way financially by marrying Julia Dallow. If he will only do this latter thing, moreover, he will promptly learn the truth of the old adage that nothing succeeds like success, for a rich old bachelor friend of his father's, a Mr. Carteret, will thereupon settle another fortune on him. And besides all this, everyone loves Nick. His mother makes no secret that he is her favorite child; Julia pines to buy the world for him; Mr. Carteret calls him his son.

Of course, they are all selfish in refusing to see what Nick's painting means to him, in not allowing him to have a life of his own apart from that of being their god, but it is hard to blame them when James makes us see so clearly that their vision of Nick's alternative to becoming a rich and revered prime minister is to be a second-rate dauber of canvases in a bohemian studio.

And finally poor Nick is by no means sure that he can paint. Is he to cause all this misery for nothing? It is a bitter thought that even if he succeeds by his own lights, his mother and Julia will never comprehend it. It is a bitterer one that he may not succeed at all. He must forfeit his expectations, alienate the woman he loves, make all for whom he cares quite wretched, and for what?

Miriam Rooth, on the other hand, at least in the beginning of her chronicle, has little alternative to becoming an actress. She must succeed or starve. She and her mother are really poor, unlike Lady Agnes Dormer who lives "in a hole," but with a butler. They must economize on fuel and even food and depend on cafés to be their sitting rooms. Miriam's mother dreams of lost gentility and imagined noble relatives, but Miriam, a realist like her deceased Jewish father, faces the world more bluntly. She perfectly comprehends her own talent — even when nobody else does — and she foresees that it will make up for everything else. She will have money, adulation, love — yes. But all these things will be as nothing to the delight she will have in her art. To have that will be the totality; to miss it will be to miss all.

I wonder if James may not have originally planned to balance Miriam's case with Nick's by giving her an alternative to the theater in the form of Peter Sherringham. Peter offers to make her an ambassadress in diamonds — a striking role, but the only one he will allow her. If, however, James ever contemplated making marriage to Peter as difficult a thing for Miriam to sacrifice as marriage to Julia is for Nick, he must have given it up as soon as Miriam's character was realized. For Miriam is the perfect type of the great actress; her whole life is a performance. In each situation that faces her she seizes at once the role that will be most rewarding to play, and she plays it dazzlingly. She is totally clear from the beginning about Peter. His proposal that she give up the stage is taken — quite properly — as an insult.

James states in the text that he has used the indirect vision for the portrayal of Miriam. Obviously, since she is a creature who is always acting, on stage or off, it is more satisfactory to see her from the point of view of her shifting audience. But when Peter, bound for a distant post in Central America, comes to bid Miriam a last farewell, we are allowed a glimpse into her mind:

> She was sorry to lose him and eager to let him know how good a friend she was conscious he had been to her. But the expression of this was already, at the end of a minute, a strange bedevilment: she began to listen to herself, to speak dramatically, to represent. She uttered the things she felt as if they were snatches of old play-books, and really felt them the more because they sounded so well. This, however, didn't prevent their really being as good feelings as those of anybody else, and at the moment her friend [Sherringham], to still a rising emotion — which he knew he shouldn't still — articulated the challenge I have just recorded, she had for his sensibility, at any rate, the truth of gentleness and generosity.

James's method of indirection will not work for a scene where Peter must be deceived by Miriam's histrionics, and the author has no resource but to assume omniscience and tell us frankly that Miriam has hardly a genuine emotion. Since she is always an actress, there is no real Miriam Rooth, only a repertory of roles. James becomes suddenly

quite stern about this. If we suspect that Peter Sherringham is something of a "male chauvinist pig" in expecting
Miriam to give up a great stage career to become a diplomat's wife, we cannot be entirely sure that James agrees
with us. However obvious it may be to him that Miriam
must be a great actress or nothing, I fancy that he thought
it a very fine thing indeed to be the spouse of a rising
diplomat in the heyday of the British Empire. There was
always a part of James's heart that thrilled to the Horse
Guards and whatever then corresponded to "Pomp and
Circumstance."

I find even less sympathetic his obvious detestation in
The Tragic Muse of everything that goes into the creation of
the magic of the theater. He shudders at the grease, the
paint, the affectations, the familiarity, the atmosphere of
easy friendship and easy sex. It is a phony world full of
phony people, and he seems to feel about it just as his
character Peter Sherringham feels: hating it most when
most drawn to it. It is ironic that after the publication of
The Tragic Muse in 1890 James was to devote five years to
an attempt to conquer the theater. It would have been
better if, like Peter, he had gone to Central America. The
theater's revenge came in 1895 when the unhappy playwright was roundly booed by the first-night audience of *Guy
Domville*.

There is really very little of great art to show from James's
long love-hate relationship with the theater except for
the stage portions of *The Tragic Muse*, and in particular
Miriam Rooth and her splendid mentor, Madame Carré.
The great scenes of the novel are those where the clumsy
but desperately determined young Englishwoman forces
herself on the attention of the aging, irritable French actress. The vitality of the story is all in the early sections, in

the evolution of Miriam into a great star. Here everything that James had observed before and behind the curtains of the Paris theater is put to the finest use. After Miriam succeeds, she becomes rather a bore. One is not as interested in her self-satisfaction when it is shared by the world as when she is a raw, passionate aspirant.

The faint ennui that affects the end of her story affects also Nick's. The interest of his career is in what he gives up. Once that is gone, he appeals to us less. James never convinces me that Nick is a great painter in the way he convinces me that Miriam is a great actress. I suspect that this is because he knew far less about painting than he knew about the stage. He was inclined to favor academic canvases; he adored Sargent; he did not appreciate the impressionists until they were fully accepted. He might have done better had he made Nick a writer, but then the example of Disraeli would have offered a compromise to Nick's problem which might have made the throwing up of his seat in the House of Commons seem quixotic. At any rate, it does not really matter. The novel deals with the conflict between the world and the arts as it affects two artists. For one of them the conflict is agony; for the other it simply does not exist.

I suppose it should not really surprise us that Nick and Miriam cease to interest us when they succeed in their chosen careers. For then they have become artists, and how can a work of art show us an artist creating a work of art? We cannot see Nick's paintings or Miriam's performances. But we can watch them starting — we can follow their struggles and sacrifices — we can see what they gain — and also what they lose. I know of no other novel where the experience is more vividly delineated.

The Ghost Stories

The ghost story is a specialized form of fiction which attracts, at one time or another in his career, almost every writer of novels and tales. Although one might have suspected that it would be disdained, or placed in the realm of the frankly commercial, this has not been the case. The ghost story has been taken very seriously indeed. When it is not merely a matter of screams and wraiths and rattled bones, it poaches quite boldly on the territory of the religious and the philosophic. Sometimes it is a bit of a fraud, pretending to an unsupported importance in linking our world with another. Sometimes it may be more than that.

Henry James had few pretensions in his ghost stories. He wanted to thrill his readers. I am not talking here about his "ghostly" tales which Leon Edel has anthologized and which include "The Altar of the Dead" where the protagonist is preoccupied with his deceased friends but not with their ghosts. By a "ghost story" I mean one either where there are actual ghosts or where the characters, for one reason or another, are made to believe that there are. The trouble with the first category is that as soon as the ghost is proved, it excites incredulousness. The trouble with the second is that as soon as it appears that the ghost is a fake or an illusion, the story collapses. That is why ghost stories are difficult to handle.

It was not for a long time a field in which James enjoyed much success. In his early career he wrote a few mild chillers, "The Romance of Certain Old Clothes," "DeGray: A Romance," and "The Ghostly Rental," the first two with a real ghost — or at least an effective posthumous malign influence — and the third with a factitious one. Later, he became more sophisticated. In "Sir Edmund Orme" the ghost of the mother's dead lover watches over the daughter to keep her from becoming another heartless jilt. He is a half-protective, half-sinister spirit, and as such is an interesting concept, but I confess to an impatience with ghosts that don't scare me. If they are inventions and fail to give me goose pimples, what are they invented for? The amiable ghost of the hanged smuggler in "The Third Person" is simply a bore. The concept of the ghost who kills the hero in "Owen Wingrave" is terrifying enough, but the horror is all confined to the final page. Up until then the story is about the troubles of a young man in a fanatical military family who refuses to go into the army. As such it is adequately interesting, but hardly a ghost story.

If James had stopped at this point, he would have had little reputation for this kind of tale. He would not have compared, for example, to his close friends Edith Wharton or Robert Louis Stevenson. But he was beginning to see what was wrong. If the whole thing in a short story was the fear, the whole concentration should be on the fear. He speaks in his preface to "The Turn of the Screw" of the dilution of terror caused by the modern "psychical" ghost story, where scientific explanation of the spirit douses the "dear old sacred terror," and he then explains the germ of his story. It was a story told to him by a "distinguished" host (actually the Archbishop of Canterbury) as they sat by the hall fire of a "grave old country-house." It concerned two small children in an out-of-the-way place haunted by the ghosts of "bad" servants who somehow wanted to "get hold of them." This was all James was told, all that his host himself had been told as a young man — this "shadow of a shadow" — and it was all that James needed. For the chill, the thrill, the *point* was there in the weird situation, dimly remembered. It had to be developed, dramatized, "caught," without being lost. The working out of the problem would be "a piece of ingenuity pure and simple, of cold artistic calculation, an *amusette* to catch those not easily caught."

James has perfectly stated here the purpose of his ghost story. Peter Quint and Miss Jessel, he explains, are not so much "ghosts" as they are "goblins, elves, imps, demons" whose villainy of motive constitutes the essence of the matter. What he happily comprehended was that any definition of that motive would inevitably dissipate the eerie atmosphere which would be the whole point of the tour de force. The "grand form of wrong-doing" should not be allowed to shrink to the compass of a "particular brutality." James then proceeded to tip his hand in the preface by admitting that he had left the definition of the evil to his reader. The job of the author was to make the reader's *general* sense of evil intense enough. The latter's own imagination would then finish the job.

Despite what strikes me as a candid statement by the author that, one, his spirits are spirits and, two, there is no

"'And hark, what songs the Seraphim do sing!' Archbishop Benson giving Mr Henry James the idea for 'The Turn of the Screw'" (Beerbohm, 1920)

rational explanation for his tale, two of his greatest critics, Edmund Wilson and Leon Edel, adhere to the theory that Peter Quint and Miss Jessel are figments of the governess's perfervid imagination. There is considerable evidence to base the theory on. In the first place, the opening of the story is shrouded in mystery. Why has it so appalled Mr. Douglas who is in possession of the manuscript? Why does he assure the others of the house party that there has never been anything like it for dreadfulness? It leads one to expect something more horrible than mere ghosts. And when the governess makes her first appearance, we realize at once that she has fallen in love with her future employer after only two interviews and is in a highly charged emotional state. The housekeeper, Mrs. Grose, an ignorant woman who cannot read or write, is easily made a prisoner of her strong imagination and comes to believe in the ghosts, even though she cannot see them. Finally, the Wilson-Edel theory tempts one because it makes the ending of the story so much more terrifying. When Flora fails to see the ghost of Miss Jessel to which her lunatic governess points, she is horrified. But she tells Miles what has happened. Mrs. Grose takes Flora away, and the poor little boy finds himself alone in the great house with a crazy woman, knowing that his turn will be next. He has done everything he could to avoid this; he has even begged to be sent off to school, but nothing has worked. Now the fiend asks him if he does not see what *she* sees. Staring at her with terror, he knows that she is doing to him what she tried to do to Flora. But he denies that he can see Miss Jessel. Then the governess tells him that it is *not* Miss Jessel that she sees, and he understands at last that it is the spirit of Quint which she is conjuring up. At this point his heart stops.

The Wilson-Edel theory of the psychotic governess thus fits with the latter's violent infatuation with her employer, with the determined, brutal way in which she cross-examines the children and the housekeeper, almost forcing them to confess to seeing things that they have not seen, and, finally, with the important fact that none of the other characters ever admits to having seen the ghosts. But there is an overwhelming objection to it. The governess, who has never seen Peter Quint in the flesh, or even heard of his existence, describes his ghost to the housekeeper with an exactitude which enables Mrs. Grose to identify the dead valet. Leon Edel claims that the governess drags the identification out of the reluctant mind of an ignorant and terrified woman, but I cannot read the passage this way, and there is no other example in James's work of this kind of suggestive questioning.

The other theory is the governess's own: i.e., that the ghosts are real and are trying to lead the children to death so that they may be the ghosts' companions in damnation. The governess's role will be to exorcise the ghosts by inducing Flora and Miles to mention their presence and to discuss them freely of the children's own accord. She fears that she will only play into the ghosts' hands if she accuses the children directly of having relations with them. Only if they "come clean" can they be saved. The literary advantage of this theory is that real ghosts are more terrifying than fantasies and that the reader feels sympathy for the governess's horrid, lonely plight and admiration for her courage in sticking to her grim task. In the end she fails, certainly with Flora, because she has called attention to Miss Jessel's ghost without waiting for Flora to admit that she has seen it. Flora, taken off by Mrs. Grose, indulges in explosions of language viler than any she could have learned at home, which is evidence, not only that she has been in contact with the ghosts, but that she has been captured by them. Whether or not Miles is saved in the end remains a question. It is he who first mentions the name of Peter Quint, but he also calls his governess a devil and dies.

It is my theory that James was conscious of both interpretations of his story and that he used the ambiguity so created as a means of avoiding the ancient dilemma of ghost-story writers. The constant suggestion that the ghosts may be the governess's illusion does not derogate from the terror which they create for the reader in the scenes where she believes that she sees them — and where we cannot help suspecting that she really may. Thus we can see Mrs. Grose in some parts of the story as shrewdly suspecting the governess's derangement and, owing to good manners or fear, pretending to accept it, and in other parts as truly convinced that the house is haunted. Or both interpretations could be true. At first skeptical, Mrs. Grose at last believes. The fact that she does not see the ghost of Miss Jessel when the governess sees it need not be a proof that it does not exist. Ghosts could always choose to whom they would appear — vide *Hamlet*. And we can see the children either as conscious of the governess's obsession or terrified that she may really see the spirits. That the reader keeps changing his mind can add to the horror, and the ending is a chiller under either theory or both. What James has done is what he said he would do: he has succeeded in scaring us. This theory has the incidental advantage of offering an explanation of why he always refused to illuminate readers who asked him to interpret the story. He couldn't!

Without taking back any of my claim that "The Turn of the Screw" represents the ultimate in the ghost story, and that its very inexplicability contributes to this end, I should like to propose "The Jolly Corner" as the perfect ghost story in the more limited area of the explained. This last of James's tales in this category (if we omit the unfinished *The Sense of the Past*) not only is tightly organized — it fits, in every particular — but is designed to create something more than simple fear. James here has a serious theme: Spencer Brydon's compulsion to find out what he might have become had he spent his life in New York instead of expatriating himself. Had he remained at home, he would

presumably have developed his strong aptitude for business. Alone, night after night, in the bare, empty family
house he roams the rooms and corridors in search of the
spirit of himself as he might have been. His eerie sense of a
ghostly presence hiding somewhere, elusive but at the
same time sinister, is to me more scary even than Peter
Quint. And the climax, when the spirit is finally cornered
and faces its pursuer raising a mutilated hand, is quite as
terrible as it should be. Brydon, as almost does the reader,
faints away.

The missing two fingers are not only the device by which
the author can show that the spirit seen by Alice Staverton
in her dream is the same as the one encountered by Brydon; they are also the symbol of the mutilation of the spirit
caused by a life dedicated to mammon. James in this fable
has used the short story to make a strong moral point. At
the end of his literary career he demonstrated that he
could go beyond the magical chiller.

The Theater Years

James in the first half of the decade of the 1890s dedicated himself primarily to the theater, abandoning the novel though adhering to the short story. The experiment, a total failure, ended with the notorious incident of the unhappy author being booed by an obstreperous audience when he appeared on the stage after the première of *Guy Domville*. Thereafter, as recorded in the magnificent passage from the notebooks, he rededicated himself with a fierce passion to his true art: "I take up my *own* old pen again — the pen of all my old unforgettable efforts and sacred struggles. To myself — today — I need say no more. It is now indeed that I may do the work of my life. And I will."

It has been commonly said by critics, including no less a one than Leon Edel, that James learned from his dramatic experiments the "scenario" approach to fiction which formed the basis of the structure of the great last novels. Certainly James believed this himself. We find him recording his gratitude to the theater again and again in his notebooks, as for example: "When I ask myself what there may have been to show for my long tribulation, my wasted years and patiences and pangs, of theatrical experiment, the answer, as I have already noted here, comes up as just possibly *this*: what I have gathered from it will perhaps have been exactly some such mastery of fundamental statement — of the art and secret of it, of expression, of the sacred mystery of structure."

It does not seem to me that an examination of James's plays and the novels which followed them will bear this out. His theater, a confused mishmash of clumsy exits and entrances and botched climaxes, constitutes precisely that portion of his work where the scenario method is least in evidence. By the scenario method I mean storytelling conceived in scenes showing characters communicating by conversation in moments of illuminating tension. Actually, the novels of the Balzac period, which predate James's theater years, particularly *The American* and *Portrait of a Lady*, are filled with just such scenes. When he dramatized *The American* he had only to lift the dialogue from his book. Yet by doing so he wrote a better play than any which followed.

The three great novels of the major phase seem to me a logical extension, not of the plays, but of James's steadily developing sense of the dramatic — as opposed to the directly theatrical — in the books of the Balzac period. What he found that he could do was to explore the communication between his characters by impressions given through the mind and eye as well as the ear. The scene in *The Golden Bowl* where Maggie wrestles in the carriage with her husband's efforts to dominate her sexually and so force her to look away from his intrigue with her step-mother is an exciting one, but it would be a deadly bore on stage or screen. For the two sit up straight, side by side, making the briefest of comments. Only in their minds and hearts does the conflict rage. To say that James owed this scene to the theater would simply be to say that he owed all items of human interest in his work to the theater — that there is no art *but* in the theater. Excitement and drama in fiction have no necessary relation to excitement and drama on the stage. *The Awkward Age* is the only major work of James that owes anything to his playwriting experiments, and that debt is only a mechanical one.

What James never learned was how to make his characters reveal themselves in dialogue. They all talk alike, and artificially. This makes no difference in the novels. There the characters are so vividly presented in the prose that we are delighted to have them speak beautifully — as if they were declaiming poetry or singing. Stylization of dialogue occurs in many of our greatest works of fiction. But when the curtain rises on a drawing room of our own day, the actors have only the vernacular in which to introduce and describe themselves. James never addressed himself to this problem. I doubt that he even recognized it. What he really wanted was to be a playwright, rather than to write plays — a common failing in novelists. If he had ever followed the instructive method of writing his first drafts without any stage notes at all, he might have seen this. Consider the following excerpt from *The Other House* where Tony, the hero, is duped by the villainess, Rose, into believing that she has just been jilted by Vidal.

TONY. (*All embarrassed and beautifully gaping, the unexpected having sprung upon him.*) Bless my soul, my dear child — you don't mean to say there *are* difficulties? (*Across the interval, as he speaks she suddenly faces round, and his view of her hereupon at once making him smite his forehead in his expressive penitent way. Something comes over him.*) What a brute I am not to have seen you're not quite happy, and not to have noticed that *he* — ! (*He catches himself up: the face offered him is the convulsed face* ROSE *has managed though only comparatively to keep from her lover. She literally glares at him; standing there with her two hands pressing down her agitated breast and something in all her aspect like the first shock of a great accident. What he sees, without at first understanding it, is the final snap of tremendous tension, the end of her wonderful false calm; which makes him instantly begin, dismayed and disappointed, to guess and spell out, as it were, quite misunderstandingly, the real truth of her situation. He thus springs at the idea that she has received a blow — a blow which her self-control up to within a moment only presents now as more touchingly borne. Her desire to get rid of* VIDAL *becomes instantly a part of it for him: what has somehow happened flashes into vividness. Thus — giving her all the benefit of it — he pieces her case together.*) His eagerness to leave you surprised me — and yours to make him go! (*Then as it still more intensely comes to him, while even before he speaks her eyes seem to glitter it back.*) He hasn't brought you bad news — hasn't failed, for you, of what we hoped? (*Going nearer for compassion and tenderness.*) You don't mean to say, my poor girl, that he doesn't meet you as you supposed he would? (*Then as she drops at his approach, into a chair, where she bursts into passionate tears, and while she throws herself upon a small table, burying her head in her arms just as* JEAN *has first found her, he stands over her, all wonder and pity, and feels helpless as she sobs.*) You don't mean to say he doesn't keep Faith?

Now read the above without stage notes.

TONY. Bless my soul, my dear child — you don't mean to say there *are* difficulties? What a brute I am not to have seen you're not quite happy, and not to have noticed that *he* — ! His eagerness to leave you surprised me — and yours to make him go! He hasn't brought you bad news — hasn't failed, for you, of what we hoped? You don't mean to say, my poor girl, that he doesn't meet you as you supposed he would? You don't mean to say he doesn't keep Faith?

James might have recognized from this experiment that one doesn't write a play simply by eliminating the prose from a novel. With his elaborate stage notes he was trying to have his cake and eat it. But even without them he does not seem to have tried to put himself in the shoes of one declaiming his lines. No actress could bring off the following, from the same play:

ROSE. Perhaps you know then that her detestable Stepmother was, very little to my credit, my Aunt. If her Father, that is, was Mrs. Griffin's second Husband, my Uncle, my Mother's brother, had been the first. Julia lost her Mother; I lost both my Mother and my Father. It was then that Mrs. Griffin took me on: she had shortly before made her second marriage. She put me at the horrid school at Weymouth at which she had already put her Stepdaughter. But it's the only good turn she has ever done us.

The characters, drained of the blood which James in fiction might have pumped into them and depending for their lives on a stylized dialogue, are mere puppets, and oddly heartless ones at that. What then of the plot and situation of the plays? Did James mean to pull out of his trap by writing the problem play so popular in the last quarter of the nineteenth century, particularly in France?

It is difficult to know just what James meant by saying that he had the French theater in his pocket, unless it was that he had attended every important theatrical presentation in Paris for a quarter of a century. He loved the climactic social dramas of Émile Augier and Dumas *fils* which bristled with such formidable examples of the decline of manners and morals in Paris high life as the intermarriage of gentlemen with whores, prostitution in the *haute bourgeoisie*, and the increasing mix-up of the *monde* with the *demimonde*. It must have seemed at times to their gaping audiences as if all the ills of the world might be cured by the *pièce à thèse*. Yet none of the four comedies in James's *Theatricals*, or *Guy Domville*, fits into this category. The four comedies deal with situations which border on farce, and *Guy Domville*, for lack of a better classification, might be called a costume drama or period piece.

The other contemporary influence on James was Ibsen, whose plays tend to fall into two categories: psychological studies of strong, highly individual characters, such as Hedda Gabler, or problem plays, covering generally a broader social plane than the French theater, such as *Ghosts* or *An Enemy of the People*. James was fascinated by Ibsen, but I can find no trace of the latter's influence in his work except in *The Other House* where Rose Armiger, the murderess, is a kind of Hedda (though she owes something to Racine, too: Phèdre, Roxane, Eryphile) and where Mrs. Beever and the doctor suggest Mrs. Alving and the pastor. Of course, too, it is possible that James considered the matter of preserving an old landmark house, as in *The High Bid*, or that of keeping master paintings out of the hands of greedy Americans, as in *The Outcry*, social problems of the Ibsen category, but if so I can only sympathize with the audience of *The High Bid* which applauded loudly when one of the characters pointed out that new housing was more needed than old landmarks. Throughout the two volumes of *Theatricals*, at any rate, which James published as the flower of his dramatic experimentation, there is no strong character of the type of Hedda Gabler and no social problem that warrants the name. In these comedies James was after a simpler goal: he wanted to make his audience laugh.

This brings us up finally against the most extraordinary thing of all in this odd chapter of his life: namely, that his comedies are the least funny things in the whole Jamesian canon. If he gave up character, if he eschewed problems of social significance, all that was really left on a stage that had not yet seen the "sex comedy" or the "mood" drama or the theater of the absurd was the drawing-room comedy, the sprightly, graceful piece where each line creates a laugh. But James's dialogue seems to depend for its kicks entirely on characters who display a mild form of impudence: imperious older ladies who order about young men and women; mock villains who candidly admit their wickedness; servants whose retorts reflect upon the inanity of their masters' demands. It is all quite deadly. Why he was so utterly unable to see that Oscar Wilde at this time was succeeding just where he failed I can ascribe only to professional jealousy. It is surely one of the perversities of literary history that the author of *The Golden Bowl* should have wasted so many years trying to write *The Importance of Being Earnest* without even recognizing what he was after.

The Revulsion from Sex:
The Awkward Age and
What Maisie Knew

I have commented on the quality of heartlessness in James's plays. They are dehumanized by reason of his inability to create characters by dialogue. But that is not the only reason. James in his theater years seems to have suffered a sort of nervous breakdown. He passed his fiftieth birthday, always a terrible milestone, and it must have seemed to him that he had attained neither the artistic nor the popular success for which he believed he had sacrificed all else. Is it possible that he came to associate his failure in the theater with the easygoing sexual habits of stage people that Peter Sherringham so deplored in *The Tragic Muse*? Did he see the wretched theater world, which had rejected *him*, spreading its contamination over the very society which had provided him with all his old subject material, as if to take *that* away from him, too? This may be highly fanciful, but sex, certainly, had begun to obsess him as an evil thing.

Up to the 1890s he had treated fornication as other contemporary writers had. He disapproved of it — decidedly — but he used it as a necessary incident in his plotting. In *The Portrait of a Lady*, though his sympathy is all for Isabel, he implied that the liaison between Gilbert Osmond and Madame Merle was something which would hardly surprise an Italian or Frenchman. Indeed, I should go so far as to surmise that James of the Balzac period, without ever posing as a boulevardier, wanted his reader to be aware that he was no raw provincial, no country cousin.

But starting with "A London Life" in 1889 a distinct note of horror at fornication enters his fiction. Laura Wing, who anticipates the hysterical governess of "The Turn of the Screw," is so appalled by her sister's adultery that she throws herself at the head of the first available young man, begging him to marry her and save her from the disgrace with which she feels herself involved. James, through one of his worldly-wise old woman characters, Lady Davenant, is careful to explain that Laura is an extreme, even an unbalanced creature. But his identification with Laura and her dismay was growing. In *What Maisie Knew* he makes his personal recoil more palatable to his reader by identifying himself with a little girl, the daughter of the adulterous couple. Even Lady Davenant would raise her hands at the sight of a child exposed to such contacts. And the reader's sympathy is again enlisted on the side of virtue in "The Turn of the Screw" where two beautiful innocents are shown as contaminated by an affair between their governess and a low, pushing valet. But James would not limit himself to the effect on children of such encounters. What would that be but to admit that fornication was morally permissible between "consenting adults"? No, he had to push his revulsion further. Sex in his fiction now becomes an evil which affects even those who only talk about it. *The Awkward Age* is the neurotic credo of this disturbed period in his life.

It should be noted at the outset of a consideration of this novel that James found sexual freedom particularly offensive in London society, his own home territory. He had learned to cope with the old English double standard of the 1870s: that either a woman was pure or she was a whore. One can speculate that James, an inhibited bachelor, probably a virgin, had made his peace easily enough with this distinction. A pure woman would never threaten him — she was safe in the ivory tower of her virginity or in the cathedral of her marriage — and a whore . . . well, who cared? But if the world — and even the society in which one moved — was to be filled with bold, demanding females, things had come to a pretty pass. A gentleman would not even be safe from advances in a drawing room!

His thesis, seriously advanced in *The Awkward Age*, is that Nanda Brookenham, a charming nineteen-year-old, kind and deep, cultivated, sensitive, exquisite in her human sympathies, can yet be disqualified as a bride for a fine young man by the soilure of her virginal freshness through exposure to the racy gossip of her mother's salon. There is not a hint that Nanda herself has become promiscuous or that she is even remotely so inclined. The knowledge alone of such things is the contamination.

There are moments in the book when James, like a softhearted Puritan, seems to quail in his dismal task. His character Mitchy, a lovable, humble, apologetic millionaire, defends Nanda in words that make the reader want to stand up and cheer: "The modern girl, the product of our hard London facts and of her inevitable consciousness of them just as they are — she, wonderful be-

"A Rage of Wonderment" — Beerbohm depicts James about 1904.
James wrote in his essay on D'Annunzio, "That sexual passion . . .
has no more dignity . . . than the boots and shoes that we see,
in the corridors of promiscuous hotels, standing,
often in double pairs, at the doors of rooms."

ing, *is*, I fully recognize, my real affair, and I'm not ashamed to say that when I like the individual I'm not afraid of the type."

But a careful reading seems to make sadly clear that James rather looks down on Mitchy, who is vulgarly *nouveau riche*. Nanda, however polluted by dirty talk, would be good enough for the likes of *him*, but she is definitely not good enough for Van, straight and blond and truly British, the perfect Victorian gentleman. Oh, it is true, James has to concede, that Van may seem a bit particular to turn his back on this lovely girl, even when a fortune is thrown in to lure him, but what the author is really telling us is that Van's particularity is a commendable survival from a better era. Indeed, James goes so far as to point out that this quality in Van is the very thing that attracts Nanda to him. For the poor girl is represented as being too sensitive not to know and despise what is wrong with her. This is made explicit in one of her last dialogues with Mitchy:

> "But what's the use," he persisted as she answered nothing, "in loving a person [Van] with the prejudice — hereditary or other — to which you're precisely obnoxious. Do you positively *like* to love in vain?"
>
> It was a question, the way she turned back to him seemed to say, that deserved a responsible answer. "Yes."

Yet for all the silliness of its thesis, *The Awkward Age* remains one of my favorites among James's novels. Like Meredith's *The Egoist* it is a brightly toned interior picture, a brilliant exercise in wit, a parlor comedy of the mind. Its structure is unique in the canon. James confined himself entirely to dialogue and to descriptions of the characters as they speak, with the result that the novel reads like the scenario of a television series. Never once do we go inside a character's mind, although there are times when the author's speculations about what a particular facial expression may imply are so elaborate as to make us wish he would drop the subterfuge and show himself as frankly the omniscient author. But for the most part we do not really need to go into the minds of the speakers. The "bad" characters, all of Mrs. Brookenham's group — herself, her husband, the duchess, Lord Petherton, the Cashmores, Harold, Tishy, Grendon — are a shallow lot bound together by their common love of what they like to call good talk, which is really only a kind of disciplined gossip about sex in society. The atmosphere about them is beautifully created by their brittle wit, their subtle facial expressions, and the reader's sense of the infinite variety of the enchanting Mrs. Brookenham, who provides the element essential (as the worldly James well knew) to hold such a group together and to give it a special tone, even a whiff of redemption. And of the "good" characters, Mr. Longdon is too simple, Nanda too transparent, to need to be penetrated. Besides, Nanda is the *donnée* of the situation, the given problem. One has to accept her without explanation. And, finally, it is imperative for the author to keep us out of Van's mind, for how else could he keep us from despising him? James dares not allow us inside that cotton puff of fatuity. So his technique works.

The most dramatic example in this period of James's antipathy to sex is *The Sacred Fount*, where the central observer at a weekend house party selects examples of couples to bear out his theory that a man and woman in a marriage or love affair can become cannibals and actually live off the partner. In this case the characters change physically as well as mentally. An older wife is seen to be rejuvenated by preying on her husband who at the same time visibly ages; another woman is deprived of wit as her lover gains it. I cannot find a redeeming feature in this unpleasant novel; I can only regard it, as did many of James's admirers at the time of its publication, as a sad aberration. Discussion if it belongs to his biographer, and I say no more of it here. The sole interest for me in James's mental depression during the middle years of the 1890s is its effect on the better books of that period. *The Awkward Age* is one of such; *What Maisie Knew*, another.

The change in the age of the person exposed to the dirty talk from Nanda's (nineteen) in *The Awkward Age* to Maisie's (twelve?) in *What Maisie Knew* eliminates most of the unpleasantness of James's prudishness. For Nanda is of an age to look after herself, without either James or Van prying into her affairs, whereas Maisie's case is altogether different. That a child should be tossed from one parent to another, from one stepparent to another, exposed all the while to their sordid quarrels and even more sordid intrigues, would arouse the concern of a domestic relations court even in our day. When Van in *The Awkward Age* is troubled that Nanda may lose her moral sense in her mother's adulterous world, we find him a prig, but when Mrs. Wix shows the same concern over Maisie, we find her a heroine.

Yet a close reading will show that *What Maisie Knew* has all the same prejudices as *The Awkward Age*. For the thing that brings about the crisis in Boulogne and that stiffens poor battered Mrs. Wix into a defiant pole of virtue, enabling her to defy Sir Claude and Mrs. Beale and take Maisie away from them, is not the low language, or the vile jealousies, or even the adultery to which the little girl has been exposed all along and which Mrs. Wix has reluctantly accepted as part of her inevitable surroundings. No, what breaks the camel's back, what produces the final revolt, is the *public* adultery of Sir Claude and Mrs. Beale. When Mrs. Wix sees Maisie in danger of accepting *this*, of being willing to live with an unwed couple, then she is ready to give Maisie up. But Maisie sees her danger and throws in her hat with Mrs. Wix. She *has*, in the end, saved her moral sense.

Now surely this is absurd, when one considers the real wickedness in the novel. Maisie's father has abandoned her, embezzled her money, and gone abroad to live off a rich woman. Maisie's mother, whose life is a succession of worthless cads, has equally thrown her over. Mrs. Wix only shakes her old head over all of this. But when Maisie's stepfather, Sir Claude, who truly loves the child, and her stepmother, Mrs. Beale, who is certainly fond of her, propose to the homeless waif that she share their French home, Maisie and Mrs. Wix flee back to England, and the novel is over. In other words, when the child is offered her first chance for love and security, it must be rejected because the persons offering it have no socially acceptable veil with which to disguise their sexual relationship — at least until their divorces are granted. Such is Mrs. Wix's "moral sense." It is easy to see that James had never been a parent.

Let us not, however, wring idle modern hands over his prejudice. It is what gives this novel its peculiar power. For Maisie and Mrs. Wix are seen as sexless creatures, lost in a world of never-ending copulation. What Maisie knows is that *that* is what grown-up people really care about — and only that. They are forever talking about it, however indirectly: their smirks, their side-glances, their sudden hilarities, even their admonitions and scoldings, are so many references to it. The moment they get out of Maisie's sight, they rush for a bed. She is almost aware of the grunts and squeals and creaking springs behind every closed door. Mrs. Wix may have once been married, but her husband (a horror, one gathers) is never referred to and her only child is dead. She has returned, so to speak, to a child's state, and she and Maisie cling to each other in the chilly hall of the vast bordello that is their universe.

They make one doomed effort to come to terms with the world of coition. Both see in Sir Claude, Maisie's step-father, a possible ally, a possible candidate, even, for membership in their sexless minority. He is kind and sympathetic, and he has been mated to Maisie's terrible mother only by a kind of rape. But to try to win him over they must use the language of sex: they must first persuade each other that they are in love with him. And their only chance for a lasting victory will be to catch him in a situation of unconcealed sexual opportunity, i.e., one where he shares a residence, even briefly, with a person not his spouse. *Then* they will be in a position to demand his renunciation of sex as a matter of right. If he agrees, he will be saved. They have a wild hope of attaining their goal when Mrs. Beale, like a hungry cat, follows Sir Claude and Mrs. Wix and Maisie across the channel. In the struggle that follows, however, Mrs. Beale wins, not because Maisie and Mrs. Wix are not strong — they have grown so, prodigiously — but because Sir Claude is "weak." That is the word, the key word, that Mrs. Wix used to describe his susceptibility to sex. He has proved himself in the end unworthy of her and Maisie, and they return without him to England to set up their own little castle against erogenous intrusions. Theirs is a weird but fascinating tale.

With *The Awkward Age* in 1899 James had gone as far as he could go in moralizing about sex. It made rather a fool out of him, as the "righteous" gunning down of the "bad" woman in *La Femme de Claude* had made a fool out of Dumas *fils*, but it had also the effect of clearing the air. After it and *The Sacred Fount* James seems to have regained his perspective in these matters. Sex in the later novels becomes more nearly what it had been before "A London Life." The neuroticism, perhaps with something as simple as James's own old age, disappeared. Strether in *The Ambassadors* learns more than a tolerance for the adultery of Chad Newsome and Madame de Vionnet. He actually becomes their champion.

The Spoils of Poynton:
Prelude to the Major Phase

I have argued that James's playwriting gave him no sub-
stantial assistance in the process of conceiving and
executing the great last novels. But there may well
have been some indirect aid. Freed from the footlights and
the impatient audiences, he may well have received a
brighter vision of the infinite capacities of the novel form.
I like to think that his great fictional talent was slowly
maturing to its final phase while he was writing the dramas
and short stories of the dramatic period. When he took up
his "old pen" again it was to pour forth a series of longer
tales in which a deeply subjective note, useless to the stage,
was richly sounded again and again. One might almost say
that James was luxuriating, triumphing in all the things
that a playwright could *not* do.

In the exquisite pages of "The Altar of the Dead" where
he describes the silent communion of his elderly protagonist in the empty chapel before the candles representing his dead friends, in the passages of "In the Cage"
where we take in the hopeless, absurd passion of the tele-

graph operator for the dissolute officer who is hardly aware of her existence, in the contrast between the pompous letters of the dead peer and the glowing love letters of his humbler friend in "The Abasement of the Northmores," I rejoice to find again not only the great artist of the Balzac period, but a heart more deeply compassionate than ever before. The miasma of the theater years, the nervous years, what Leon Edel has so rightly called the treacherous years, is being slowly blown away.

The Spoils of Poynton, much more than James's dramas, seems to me the true link between his Balzac period and his major phase, the direct precursor of the two great novels which were so soon to follow it: *The Wings of the Dove* and *The Golden Bowl*. At the very beginning of *The Spoils* we see James making the transfer from his old fashion of allocating points of view to his new and final one. He tells us directly that Fleda Vetch is "that member of the party in whose intenser consciousness we shall most profitably seek a reflection of the little drama with which we are concerned." She has the same intense consciousness of Maggie in *The Golden Bowl* and all of her moral fineness. Yet her situation borrows a little from that of a very different character, Kate Croy in *The Wings of the Dove*. Like Kate, Fleda has a father in London who will not have anything to do with her and an older sister who is the fiancée (rather than the widow) of a dreary curate and who looks upon Fleda as a person whose sole function in life is to help her out. Unable to exist with either of these, Fleda comes under the protection of Mrs. Gereth, as Kate comes under the protection of Aunt Maud Lowder. Mrs. Gereth's acquisition of beautiful things is reminiscent of Adam Verver's amassing of his great collection. There is even a scene where Owen, an engaged man, tries to buy Fleda a present in a shop, just as Amerigo does for Charlotte in *The Golden Bowl*. But the most essential quality that *The Spoils* shares with *The Golden Bowl* and *The Wings of the Dove* is the study of evil as a failure of sensitivity, as a failure, almost, of taste.

For, as with the "villains" of the major phase, there is nothing wicked in the three characters with whom Fleda is involved: Mrs. Gereth, Owen Gereth, and Mona Brigstock. Mrs. Gereth, it is true, has been somewhat dehumanized by her love of possessions, but she is still a magnificent, acutely intelligent creature who embellishes the universe around her and does no harm to anyone who does not step between her and her bric-a-brac. Mona is an unsympathetic girl, but one feels in the fierceness of her determination to have Poynton refurnished with the objects of which it has been despoiled a basic and understandable antagonism to a dangerously aggressive future mother-in-law. As for Owen, he is simply an amiable, unimaginative man who does not know how to get out of an unfortunate and impulsive engagement. Fleda's role is to demonstrate the effect (or lack thereof) on these worldly characters of a deep moral sensitivity. They cannot comprehend it. Owen deserts her; Mona insults her; Mrs. Gereth considers her a fool. Fleda's good must be her sole reward.

Many readers have found Fleda too sensitive. Why can she not allow her situation to work itself out to a happy conclusion? If Mrs. Gereth will only hang on to the beautiful furnishings, the "spoils," which she has ravished from her son's house — all of which were acquired through her own genius as a collector — then Mona will break her engagement, and Owen and Fleda will happily marry. But no. Fleda must insist that Owen make a clean break with-

out the aid of any such device. Nobody, she argues, has a
right to get off easily from pledges "so deep and sacred."

It has even been pointed out by some critics that Fleda
may be morally wrong in sending Owen back to a fiancée
whom he dislikes. But first, we should remember that an
engagement, even in the later Victorian era, was not considered a testing period but a commitment only slightly
less binding than the exchange of vows at an altar. The
whole plot of George Meredith's *The Egoist* depends on
this assumption. Secondly, we should look closely on just
what it is that Fleda does. She not only is willing to listen to
Owen's declaration but admits freely that she returns his
sentiment. She makes it entirely clear that she will marry
him if and when he is free. Having done this, she firmly
dismisses him until such time as he can tell her that he *is*
free. It is up to him to withdraw from his engagement.

I fail to see why, even today, this is not the honorable
way to proceed. I also concede that it is the way to lose a
weak man. Torn between a woman who is willing to make
scenes and a woman who is not, he will obviously become
the property of the former. But that is precisely the problem posed by the novel. Fleda is not supposed to be a
sensible or a practical creature. She represents not only
what is finest in human sensitivity, but the fate of a sensitive person in a world of rougher perceptions. She can feel
all the beauty of the spoils of Poynton without letting them
dominate her as they dominate Mrs. Gereth, and she can
entertain a passion for Owen without losing sight of what
she deems her duty. In the end, she will be left without the
spoils and without Owen.

In the situations which James was later to create for
Milly Theale and for Maggie Verver, he avoided the pitfall
of having his reader become impatient with his heroine.

We can feel only the deepest sympathy for Maggie, who finds that her husband is making love to her stepmother, and only the deepest pity for Milly, who finds herself in love with a man who hopes to become her rich widower. But Maggie triumphs in life, and Milly in death. Neither has the desolate fate of Fleda who is left to contemplate the ashes of a life which must at some times seem, even to her, the result of her own perversity. Fleda, like Strether in *The Ambassadors*, "gets" nothing out of her story. But Strether can at least go home with the sense of a new awareness. Fleda is the most unrewarded of heroines. It makes her one of my favorites.

The "Villains"
of the Major Phase

The plots of *The Golden Bowl* and *The Wings of the Dove* are bizarre, even exotic. An Italian prince and a beautiful American girl, too poor to wed each other, marry instead an American heiress and her tycoon father, and continue their intrigue. An English journalist and a beautiful English girl, too poor to wed each other, agree that the journalist shall marry a dying American heiress, inherit her money, and then wed his true love. How often does one meet these situations in life?

Not often. But that only intensifies their interest. James had learned that the heavy weight of his detailed analyses of human consciousness needed a strong central pillar of interest in his readers. In *The Sacred Fount* that pillar had been too slender. It was difficult for readers to accept his central thesis that some people actually consume others, that they live physically at these others' expense. Equally unacceptable, in *The Awkward Age*, was the notion that a young girl can be soiled for the hero by her exposure to the racy conversation of her mother's social circle. But the

123

agony of a woman who finds her husband making a cuck-
old of her adored father, or that of one, dying, who discovers that her beloved is looking forward to the probate
of her will, is not apt to be dull. The situations are like
those in the tragedies of Corneille — brothers who slaugh-
ter blaspheming sisters, mothers who demand the heads of
daughters-in-law — unusual, macabre, but lively. The
sense of the Minotaur waiting in the center keeps the pris-
oners of the maze alert.

Also, as in Corneille, whose villains have qualities of the
heroic — Cleopatre, Attila — the villains of these two
novels are not evil in a conventional sense. While it is certainly true that in *The Golden Bowl* the word "evil" is spe-
cifically used at several points, both by the author and by his
representative, Fanny Assingham, to describe the intrigue
of the prince and Charlotte, I do not recall any instance in
either novel where it is set forth explicitly that the two
mentioned lovers, or the two conspirators in *The Wings of
the Dove*, Kate Croy and Merton Densher, are actually
"evil" people. The closest we come to it is where Merton
Densher uses the term "hound" to delineate Lord Mark
for harboring the same designs on Milly Theale's fortune
that he is harboring, and even here he seems more to be
describing the grossness of Lord Mark's approach than his
motive.

It is important to note that these four characters —
Prince Amerigo, Charlotte Stant, Kate Croy, and Merton
Densher — have two things in common: they are all poor,
at least at the start of their chronicles, and they all take for
granted that matrimony offers them the only possible escape from their poverty. Now it seems unlikely that James
considered the second point as having much bearing on
the goodness or badness of their characters. Prince

Amerigo, of ancient lineage, high style, and personal beauty, is obviously unqualified for the marketplace, and the fact that Merton Densher, a clever journalist and an intellectual to his fingertips, can never picture himself as earning any large sum is presented as almost a virtue. And certainly James, at the turn of the century, did not expect women — at least women brought up to be ladies — to work. So we are brought back, in rating their goodness or badness, to the poverty of the two couples. It seems that James considered poverty as an essential part of the evil in which they are involved.

Certainly he connected virtue with wealth — wealth inherited, or, in rare cases, wealth worthily accumulated, as by Adam Verver. James makes the point again and again that Milly Theale is inseparable from her money. "She couldn't dress it away, nor walk it away, nor read it away, nor think it away; she could neither smile it away in any dreamy absence nor blow it away in any softened sigh. She couldn't have lost it if she had tried — that was what it was to be really rich. It had to be *the* thing you were." Could Scott Fitzgerald have put it more bluntly? And Maggie Verver's fortune gives her so definite a moral superiority over Charlotte that even after Charlotte marries her father, thus obtaining equal wealth and rank, her old friend continues to defer to her. It is clear that whatever virtue adheres to money, it cannot be acquired by words uttered at an altar.

Must one, therefore, in a Jamesian world, be born rich in order to be really good? In a way, yes. For James, in Milly and Maggie, was engaged in painting the portraits of two souls as exquisite and fine as any he could possibly conceive, and yet at the same time as charming — that was the real trick. Could a soul that was subject to the demeaning harassments of poverty and the trials of envy have quite the same fineness, quite the same *charm*, as one that was not? James did not have to be concerned with the justice or injustice of this. Beauty of soul, like beauty of feature, might be the gift of capricious gods. Still, one recognized it when one saw it. Was not the beauty and innocence of America — to nineteenth-century eyes — inextricably bound up with her natural riches? The American dream, like Milly and Maggie, could hardly exist in our imagination without its counterpart of an envious greed beamed from the eyes of an ancient Europe.

Virtue and wealth, therefore, are opposed to poverty and evil. Yet, as already pointed out, the perpetrators or causers of the evil need not be evil themselves. James goes to great pains in *The Wings of the Dove* to make a moral case for Kate Croy and Merton Densher. Both are sincerely devoted to Milly Theale, the girl whose money they are after. They want to make her last months as happy as possible. How can she be happier than by marrying Densher, whom she has always loved? Kate tactfully withdraws so that Milly may have him to herself for as long as may be. The conspirators are not miserly. They do not count the days.

But what Kate fails to understand is that her plot is a violation of the deepest sincerity in human relationships. Kate, like Lord Mark, like most of the English, in Milly's view, is devoid of any real imagination. She has the fancy to conceive her plot but not the imagination to see why it cannot work. The real reason for her compatibility with her Aunt Maud Lowder, "Britannia of the Market Place," is that they are basically so alike. Kate wants the same life that Aunt Maud wants, the large, rich, ordered existence of Lancaster Gate, but she wants more, too. She wants what Densher represents to her, "all the high dim things she lumped together as the mind." Densher will be the cream on the top of her bottle of life; through him she will have more than Mrs. Lowder. The truth is that Kate is greedier than her aunt. She wants Lancaster Gate plus culture. But she is at all times, even at the end, even in defeat, perfectly prepared to accept the responsibility and the consequences of her acts. Kate has a hard side to her nature, but she is always a good sport. Perfectly conceived to play her curious role, she never loses our sympathy.

Densher, as a character, is less successful. It is difficult for James to keep him from seeming the utter cad which the plot makes of him. But he does his best. Densher is shown, to begin with, as passionate and frustrated, so that Kate's offer of her body at the climax of her plotting can be supposed to be a powerful inducement to him to do as she prescribes. Then, too, she has taken advantage of his sympathy for a dying girl to jockey him into habits of kindness which he can hardly shut off — when he finally takes in the full horror of Kate's scheme — without endangering Milly's very life. And finally Susie Stringham, Milly's devoted companion, is willing to push Densher into Milly's arms at any price. She does not care about his motive. She only wants her friend to die happy. But despite all these pleadings Densher's honor still ends in tatters. We would think more of him if he were enough of a brute to play his part better and at least convince Milly that he and Kate were not in league.

The trouble is that Densher, as introduced by James, is not the kind of man who would make love to a dying girl for her money. Why then did James not pick a type who would have? Because such a type could never have won the love of two such women as Kate and Milly. James did not want to write the story of the victimization of a great and good woman by a shoddy adventurer. He had something far richer and subtler in mind.

The Wings of the Dove represents the pinnacle of James's prose — Densher, hounded by guilt, roaming the streets of a storm-lashed Venice, Milly turning her face to the wall in her great gilded shell of a palazzo — but *The Golden Bowl* is the perfect novel. For James has here corrected the miscalculation he made with Densher. Prince Amerigo, his counterpart, is perfectly designed for his amiably mercenary role.

What James has essentially done in *The Golden Bowl* is to bring his two opposing entities — the morally exquisite and the morally nearer normal — closer together. The "good" characters are slightly less "good" and the "bad" are less "bad." Adam Verver, a "good" character, marries Charlotte Stant in order that his daughter Maggie need not worry about his being lonely. He is perfectly frank with Charlotte about this, and it is quite in the cards, after all, that Charlotte, a poor girl with no prospects, will be satisfied with a great fortune and an art collection as substitutes for love. But even so, is his offer not a selfish one? Is he not making use of Charlotte? And Maggie, the other "good" character, who freely allows her handsome Italian husband to escort her beautiful stepmother to all the London parties so that she may devote her evenings to her father — is she not being fatuous to the point of irresponsibility? Adam and Maggie, blind in their mutual fondness, create a situation where adultery is bound to rear its head.

The badness of the "bad" characters, on the other hand, consists largely in their failure to disclose to their *sposi* that they have been previously in love. Yet what does this amount to in the prince's case? Was he obliged to tell his

fiancée of his previous amours? And would he not have
been an officious prude to destroy Charlotte's one chance
to make a great match? Indeed, the prince has almost no
taint of badness. Even his adultery takes place under circumstances where continence, certainly to an Italian,
would have amounted almost to an admission of impo-
tence. And in Charlotte's case, it must be pointed out that
she does offer Adam Verver the opportunity to read the
prince's telegram, the contents of which would have dished
her marriage. Still, she knows how tactful a gentleman
she is dealing with; she is fairly sure that he will not look.
Her marrying a man while she is in love with his son-in-law
may be accounted a fault. But she means well. It is only
when she finds herself constantly flung with the prince
that she decides to take advantage of her situation. She
tries to persuade herself that Maggie will not mind.

Charlotte has another flaw. She is untouched by Maggie,
as Kate Croy is untouched by Milly. In the last analysis, a
contrast between two women is the base of each novel: a
woman of exquisite feeling and a woman of clay. One
might say that the tragedy of each situation is in the
women of clay's failure to be more than just that. Charlotte, like Kate Croy, is brave and high-minded and compe-
tent. She is more intellectual and more curious than Kate,
and also less mercenary. She cares for nothing really but
love. But she cannot rise to a great challenge. She cannot
give up the prince, as Kate in the end cannot give up the
money and marry a poor Densher. Charlotte is punished
for her badness by being sent off, like Oscar Wilde's bad
Americans, to America. Kate has told Densher in the beginning: "I shall sacrifice nobody and nothing, and that's
just my situation, that I want and that I shall try for everything." She does try, but she fails. She ends with nothing.

James's peculiar requirement for a novel in the late style was a moral situation that could bring out the fundamentals in the eternal conflict between the utterly civilized soul and its less than utterly civilized counterpart. There had to be an exquisitely sensitive protagonist to represent the good and cultivated man at his highest and best: Strether in *The Ambassadors*, Maggie in *The Golden Bowl*, Milly in *The Wings of the Dove*, and, for each of these, a group of antagonists: the Newsome family, Prince Amerigo and Charlotte, Kate and Densher, who represent, as we have seen, not so much evil as the state of mind of more ordinary mortals who cannot rise to the same peaks of feeling because their powers of vision and of love are obstructed by selfishness. The conflict so engendered creates evil which can only be overcome by the love of the protagonist.

Once this situation has been conceived, it is worked out in terms of the rational thinking and refined consciousness of the small parcel of human beings directly involved. There is no room for streams of consciousness or irrelevant thoughts or fantasies, for daydreams or for any hint of the id or of the subconscious. The characters think exclusively of the principal problem in its every aspect, but we only see them thinking about it rationally as it unfolds itself to their reaching consciousness. The problem, in other words, is stripped of all irrelevancies. But having stripped it to the purest essence, James then reclothes it in splendid imagery. It and its human reflectors are seen against backgrounds whose gorgeousness provides a proper outlet for his magnificent prose.

These backgrounds have misled some critics into thinking that James has something pertinent to say about wealthy, leisured people at the turn of the century. But any sociological interest that he seems to have had in the phenomenon of a leisure class was left behind in his Balzac period. Maggie and Milly are rich and live among rich people merely that the moral beauty of their resolutions may be viewed against the sumptuousness of a great English country place or a great London house or a great Venetian palace. James owed far more to the scenic art than to the theater, and the novels of his late style are like stained-glass windows that embellish and enshrine their teachings in rich and glorious color. His contrast of the beauty of the external setting with the beauty of the inward spirit may have been what E. M. Forster had in mind when he referred to the "unique aesthetic effect" of the late novels.

Edith Wharton relates in her autobiography that she found these later novels of James's, for all their profound moral beauty, too severed from the thick, nourishing human air in which men live and move. She tells how she asked James once: "What was your idea in suspending the four principal characters in *The Golden Bowl* in the void? What sort of life did they lead when they were not watching each other, and fencing with each other? Why have you stripped them of all the human fringes we necessarily trail after us through life?" James, understandably upset by her tactless question, replied: "My dear—I didn't know I had!" After long cogitation on this question I come down on James's side. It seems to me that I know the characters in *The Wings of the Dove* and in *The Golden Bowl* even more intimately than I know the characters in the earlier novels of his Balzac period. I may have some slight difficulty in picturing how the least finely conceived of the quartet in *The Golden Bowl*, Adam Verver, might act in various situations to which he is not exposed in the novel, but I think I can picture the other three, and in particular the prince, under almost any imaginable circumstances. It is true that we do not see Maggie or Charlotte brushing her teeth but what would be gained if we did? And even that objection will be removed when we come to *The Ambassadors*. For in Chester one almost does see Strether brushing his teeth.

The Virtuous Attachment:
The Ambassadors

I first read *The Ambassadors* when I was a sophomore at Yale, and last as I approached the age of its hero: fifty-five. I found that over the years Lambert Strether had improved in my esteem. It was not that I had not initially liked him. But at nineteen I was inclined to find him a little naive and rather bumbling. I deplored his losing his rich fiancée and the security for his old age over so minor a question of principle as whether or not a rich young man should give up his idle expatriate existence and go home to the family business. But today I find myself more identified with the Parisian convert who renounces Mrs. Newsome and all her tribe, and I can even comprehend his theory of the "virtuous attachment." This, it may be remembered, was Strether's highly personal interpretation of the relationship between the handsome, virile Chad Newsome and the beautiful, seductive Madame de Vionnet.

It will be helpful to recall the steps leading up to Strether's adoption of his theory. James's protagonist is a childless widower of high ideals but small experience, of deep sensitivity but starved imagination, who has spent a mildly useful, mildly wasted life editing a quarterly magazine in Woollett, a Massachusetts manufacturing town, and acting as cultural prime minister to Mrs. Newsome, the awesome widow who owns both town and quarterly. As the novel opens, he is on his way to Paris to rescue her son Chad from a presumably low entanglement and bring him home to play his proper role in the family affairs. Mrs. Newsome's hand in marriage and a comfortable evening of life are to be Strether's reward — if he prove successful.

Once in Paris, however, Strether's imagination begins at last to find its long-needed nourishment. It does not need much. He feels no compulsion to make himself expert in matters of art or architecture or history. He simply takes in the sights and sounds and scents of the French capital as they strike him on his leisurely round. The smallest things delight him: a watery beer at a sidewalk café, a stroll in the courtyard of his small hotel, watching a young man idly smoking on the balcony, noting the way another enters a theater box after the lights are down. Paris comes in through Strether's every pore, and Chad Newsome and his enchanting companion, Madame de Vionnet, love his openness to it and the benignity that he brings to his contemplation of it — and them.

But this vision of Paris is fatal to his mission. Strether finds Chad not at all depraved but wonderfully changed for the better. He is a thoroughly civilized and delightful young man with charming looks and manners and a host of admirable friends. And who has accomplished this miracle but the very friend in whom Woollett has seen the incarnation of vice? Strether, after much soul searching, tears up his instructions and begs Chad *not* to go home.

It is not simply that he wants Chad to spend his life as an elegant boulevardier. It is that Strether's vision of Paris has given him a new vision of Woollett. He has always been aware of the greed and chicanery that were at the roots of the Newsome fortune. But what he now sees is the denial of life and beauty that underlies the arid consciences of Mrs. Newsome and her daughter Sarah. Their failure to see anything but vileness in Madame de Vionnet, or meretriciousness in the French capital, is also their failure to make anything out of the business of human existence but the few paltry rules of what they choose to call right and wrong. They are children; they play at living. Paris becomes fresh air to Strether and Woollett a vacuum, and his idea of what Chad must be saved from is precisely reversed.

Yet Chad, ironically enough, has been going through just the opposite experience. He has had his fill of Paris and is already weary of his liaison. The family business now tempts his idle mind; he is almost ready to go home. His sister, who succeeds the defaulting Strether, knows her brother better than does the ambassador whom she replaces. She sees that Chad basically belongs to Woollett and that he will grace the family company and serve successfully on the boards of local cultural institutions. What future, after all, is there for him in Paris playing second fiddle to a married woman? So Strether, it turns out, has lost all for nothing. All, that is, but the vision of the richer possibilities of life that Paris has opened up to him. The novel ends on the bleak hope that this vision will sustain him in the long aftermath in Woollett without Mrs. Newsome and her quarterly.

One can readily see from this outline that James's ticklish question was how to square his hero's New England conscience. For such a man as Strether is not going to tell Chad to throw over home and mother for a French countess without something to hang his inner monitor on. It was to answer this that James invented the theory of the "virtuous attachment." Chad's friend little Bilham, seeing that Strether adores everything about Chad's French life except the central fact that Chad is sleeping with a married woman ten years older than he, deliberately deceives Strether by telling him that it is a platonic relationship. Everyone else promptly joins in this amiable conspiracy of mild deceit, and Strether, adding the fervent wish to what he considers the beautiful thought, happily adopts the theory. Ultimately, he encounters Chad and Madame de Vionnet in a secluded country spot under circumstances that do not permit the survival of his illusion, but this is only after he has irrevocably broken with Sarah and lost forever his Woollett future.

Now this, when I was a sophomore, seemed to me to make Strether a bit of an ass. Could a man of his age really for a minute believe that the relationship between a healthy American male of twenty-eight and a beautiful, sophisticated French countess would be apt to be "virtuous"? Certainly none of the Paris characters think so. And James even shows what he himself thinks in the laughing rejoinder given by Miss Barrace to Strether's quesion about Chad and Madame de Vionnet, which she deliberately misconstrues as addressed to the "virtue" of the attachment existing between herself and a particular gentleman: "Ah, don't rob it of *all* romance!" Strether's position is ludicrous. Why in God's name should Chad stay on in Paris, giving up career, home, and marriage to dance attendance on an older woman who won't even go to bed with him?

Yet the years have taught me how desperately human beings, particularly in later life, can try to fool themselves. Strether has fallen in love with Paris and with the love that exists between Chad and Madame de Vionnet. He has never felt such exaltation before, and it is necessary for him to put it on some kind of a basis that he can understand. There is in him a stubborn, transcendental idealism that, if quixotic, is still finer than the coarser idealism of Mrs. Newsome. For all the latter's high-mindedness, she is quick to assume that Madame de Vionnet is not even the apology for a decent woman. Strether wears his New England conscience with a difference. Where Mrs. Newsome tends to condemn, he tends to extenuate. Because he sees Chad made over by a wonderfully civilized woman, he must reject the idea that they could have the kind of liaison that he has always associated with less wonderful changes in young men. To put things in his own special kind of high order he must adopt the premise that the attachment is virtuous.

It is pathetic, it is ridiculous, it is untrue. Yet, it is all the same an integral and lovable part of Strether's way of thinking and of his amiable sublimity. He has to blind himself to believe it, but he is surrounded by friends who love him and want him to be pleased. They play along with his curious delusion. But as soon as he has seen Chad and Madame de Vionnet in the country, he knows the game is up, and he casts his little theory away in good spirit, if ruefully, even conceding that he has been an old fool. And it does not make any difference in his decision. He still advises Chad that he should not desert the woman who has so transformed him. He prefers Chad in adultery to Chad in Woollett. He does not care that the young man may be giving up a career to remain tied to the apron strings of his

French mistress. But if this seems a little strong, even to the modern reader, there *is* an extenuating circumstance. Strether knows that Chad will go back. He simply wants him to stay a little longer, to stay as long as he can, to spare Madame de Vionnet as much as possible of the agony that is inevitably in store for her. There will be plenty of time for Woollett.

Strether's own future, as envisioned in the final chapter, should theoretically not be bleak. After all, he is possessed of a new philosophy of life's possibilities. But both at nineteen and at fifty-five it seemed to me that this was going to be rather cold comfort for a lonely, aging man in Woollett, on a small income, deprived of the patronage of the Newsomes. Why must he go back? James himself seems to waver for a moment on this. Maria Gostrey, the infinitely sympathetic old maid who knows everything about Americans in Europe and who has fallen in love with Strether, offers him her hand and her beautiful little apartment in Paris. Why should he not take them? For no reason except that he is a character and she a novelist's device, what James calls a *ficelle*. Her role is to elicit facts and opinions from Strether for the instruction of the reader. She cannot marry him because she does not really exist. James sternly thrusts aside the poor *ficelle* who has struggled out of her category and sacrifices Strether to the perfect symmetry of his most perfect plot.

James's Literary Use
of His American Tour

I n 1904 Henry James recrossed the Atlantic to his native America for the first time in two decades. He was
sixty-two years of age and eager to make a new assessment of the distant homeland which had never been far
from his heart or mind. He was even a bit afraid that he
might have been harsh in his younger judgments of it. He
had felt, on leaving the United States, that its civilization
was too simple, too unsophisticated, too ingenuous to provide the spiritual ambience for a major novelist of manners. America would not be ready for James until it had
produced a Thackeray, and *he* was going to be that Thackeray. But Europe in many ways had failed him, too.
There was a vulgarity in Edwardian London which contrasted unfavorably with the dark, dense, mid-Victorian
city to which the "passionate pilgrim" had emigrated so
long before. James wondered now if the American values
which he had found so pale might not have flourished in
his absence.

He was in for a disappointment. The shock of the impact upon his senses of the huge, brash, pushing American civilization (if that word does not beg the very question he had come to put) remained with him ever after. While in a few places, particularly in New England, there had survived some reminders of the charming and ordered past which seemed now, in contrast to the general rubble of demolition, even more charming and ordered, the prevailing note was of the present — a glittering, meretricious present about to crumble before an even more glittering, meretricious future. The people seemed to care for nothing but making money. They destroyed their landmarks; they polluted their fields and forests; they filled the thin, blue air with their spectral superstructures. And when they *did* make money, they could think of nothing to do with it but build tasteless, derivative palaces, huddled pointlessly together on the small lawns of fashionable watering places. James was glad to get back to England and Lamb House.

For the rest of his life, however, he was to be passionately concerned with the impressions collected on this trip. For were they not proof that the greatest decision that he had ever had to make — the abandonment of his homeland — had been the correct one? Anything so important had to be worked into his fiction, and if it could not be, then into some other literary form.

James's first attempts were in three short stories, "A Round of Visits," "Julia Bride," and "Crapy Cornelia." In all of these the American experience is insufficiently digested, as shown by the rather crude satire, which has some of the same shrill note that we find in Edith Wharton's later fiction. In "A Round of Visits," Mark Monteith, returning to New York after an absence of many years, finds it impossible to locate, among his chattering, self-

"'The Jolly Corner'" — James meets the ghost of himself as he would have been had he never left America (Beerbohm, 1908)

obsessed Manhattan acquaintances, a single ear into which he can pour the sad story of his financial ruin. In "Julia Bride" a New York debutante breaks six engagements only to find that she has disqualified herself to be the bride of the one man whom she really cares about. And in "Crapy Cornelia" a middle-aged bachelor, returning like Mark Monteith to a long-abandoned New York, finds himself so disillusioned with his native city that he spends all his evenings reminiscing about his childhood with a faded old maid.

It was not until "The Jolly Corner" that James dealt with the American experience with a firm hand. Here he abandoned petty bickering and aimed his gun at what he conceived to be the basic evil in the heart of the American scene. Spencer Brydon is again a returning expatriate, but unlike his predecessors, he possesses a true affiliation with modern New York. He has a talent for business and a devouring curiosity to know how he would have fared had he remained in the American world of competition. He prowls the old deserted family mansion at night in search of the ghost of the man he would have been had he stayed at home. When he comes upon it, the vision is shattering. The specter has a hard, vulgar, soulless look, and one of its hands lacks two fingers. As it approaches Brydon as if to assault him, the latter faints away to awaken in the happy consciousness of what he has escaped. As noted in an earlier chapter, the missing fingers presumably represent the loss of moral and aesthetic sensitivity which would have resulted from an American business career. Spencer Brydon now knows that he was quite right to go abroad.

The story has a very nasty implication, which is that Spencer Brydon is a bigger man for having spent his life as a dilettante in Europe than he would have been if he had

spent it as a successful man of affairs at home. America, in
other words, is to be avoided at almost any price. For note
that Spencer Brydon bears no resemblance to Henry
James. James always emphasized that his own temperament made even an understanding of (let alone a commitment to) business matters impossible. Very likely he did
the right thing for his literary genius in taking it to what he
deemed the more hospitable air of England. But to deduce
from his own very special case that a man of business ability and inclinations would do better to stroll the boulevards
of Paris than put them to use in New York is a pretty
strong indictment of Wall Street. Yet the story, based as it
is upon James's real feelings and not upon surface irrita-
tions, is a great one.

In the novel he left unfinished at his death, *The Ivory
Tower*, James was still experimenting with the impressions
of his American tour and the problems of the repatriated.
The hero, Graham Fielder, a cultivated but idle young
American who has spent his whole life in Europe, is sum-
moned back to his native shores by his dying uncle, a
self-made millionaire. The latter has decided to bequeath
his fortune to this hitherto unknown nephew, provided
only that the latter demonstrate that he knows nothing of
and cares nothing about money. Only thus, the old man
has oddly concluded, can he make up to society for his
own rapacity. Fielder turns out to be precisely what his
uncle has looked for. He is virgin to the world of business
and brings nothing to the job of managing money but an
immense goodwill and the boundless imagination of all
Jacobite heroes.

In the surviving fragment of the novel we see America
as it strikes Graham Fielder on his arrival at his uncle's
house in Newport. There is a vivid sense conveyed of the

bright sea and summer air and the great, crazy, overdeco-
rated "villas," but the keenest impression is of the various
people that the hero meets. For the first time in James's
fiction, these are seen essentially in terms of national
characteristics. Their Americanism almost swallows them
up. Yet the effect is as remarkable as anything that James
ever achieved.

Here is the uncle's trained nurse whose breezy intimacy
constitutes Fielder's initiation to the house:

> Miss Mumby had been to Europe, and he saw soon enough
> how there was nowhere one could say she hadn't gone and noth-
> ing one could say she hadn't done — one's perception could
> bear only on what she hadn't become; so that, as he thus per-
> ceived, though she might have affected Europe even as she was
> now affecting *him*, she was a pure negation of its having affected
> herself, unless perhaps by adding to her power to make him feel
> how little he could impose on her.

On the porch Fielder meets Abel Gaw, his uncle's old
business rival, waiting in vulturine expectancy for the meal
of figures setting forth what the estate will amount to. James
always complained that he could not "do" business figures
because he knew nothing of their affairs. How idle a worry
this was can be seen from this description of Gaw:

> . . . a little man encountered on one of his turns of the veran-
> dah and who, affecting him at first as a small waiting and watch-
> ing, an almost crouching gnome, the neat domestic goblin of
> some old Germanic, some harmonised, familiarised legend, sat
> and stared at him from the depths of an arrested rocking-chair
> after a fashion nothing up to then had led him to preconceive.
> This was a different note from any yet, a queer, sharp, hard
> particle in all the softness . . .

Gussie Bradham, seen not by Fielder but by Gaw's
daughter, is the perfect type of the American society ma-
tron with her "wondrous bloom of life and her hard

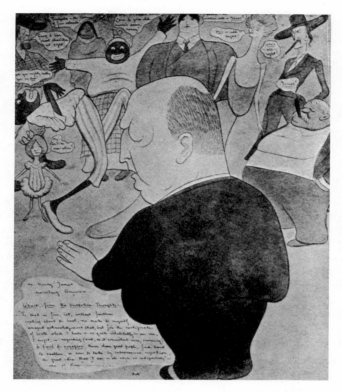

"Mr Henry James revisiting America: *Extract from His Unspoken Thoughts*. . . . 'So that, in fine, let, without further beating about the bush, me make to myself amazed acknowledgement that, but for the certificate of birth which I have — so quite indubitably — *on* me, I might, in regarding (and, as it somewhat were, overseeing) *à l'oeil de voyageur*, these dear good people, find hard to swallow, or even to take by subconscious injection, the great idea that I am — oh, ever so indigenously! — one of them' . . ." (Beerbohm, 1905) The Americans in the background are saying, left to right: "My! Ain't he cree-ative?" "We wants yer mightly badly. Yas, we *doo*!" "Guess 'e ken shoot char'cter at sight!" "Hail, great white novelist! Tuniyaba — the Spinner of fine cobwebs!" "Why, it's Masser Henry! Come to your old nurse's arms, honey!" "What's — the matter with — *James*?" "He's — all — right!" "*Who's* — all — right?" "*James!*"

confidence that had nothing to do with sympathy."
Rosanna Gaw cannot even dislike her:

. . . such a state of the person wasn't human, to the younger
woman's sombre sense, but might have been that of some shin-
ing humming insect, a thing of the long-constricted waist, the
minimised yet caparisoned head, the fixed disproportionate eye
and tough transparent wing, gossamer guaranteed.

Best of all is the description of Mr. Crick, the driest of all
dry Yankee lawyers who drearily supervises the passage of
property from the dead to the living:

The refusal of his whole person to figure as a fact invidiously
distinguishable, that of his aspect to have an identity, of his eyes
to have a consciousness, of his hair to have a colour, of his nose
to have a form, of his mouth to have a motion, of his voice to
consent to any separation of sounds, made intercourse with him
at once extremely easy and extraordinarily empty; it was deprived of the flicker of anything by the way and resembled the act
of moving forward in a perfectly-rolling carriage with the blind
of each window neatly drawn down.

James's notes for the unfinished book reveal that
Graham Fielder is to be tricked out of his fortune by the
friend to whose hands he has confided it and that he will
rise magnificently above the swindle, relieved to be rid of
his pirate's loot. We do not know what happens to him
afterwards. Presumably he goes back to Europe. James
may have been working around to the conclusion of "The
Jolly Corner." Not only is it better that the hero should not
be an American businessman; it is better that he should
not have an American business fortune. Perhaps the only
really safe thing is to live in Europe with the aid of a small,
respectable trust fund, one that dates far enough back to
be free of the smirch of modern mercantilism.

In *The Ivory Tower* some of the triviality of the satire of
the three American stories seems to have affected the

central theme. On the other hand, the observation of the American characters is vastly strengthened over that of the stories. James, in dealing fictionally with the material of his American tour, had been unable to unite a strong theme with strong treatment.

Much more successful was his volume of travel reminiscences, *The American Scene*, a brilliant combination of prose that rises to the level of poetry and language that contains his most convoluted and intricate sentences. James in his book shows himself something of a prophet. There are passages where he foretells nothing less than the current destruction of our environment and the horrors of ethnic struggles. It is astonishing how much he was able to make out of a countryside viewed from the moving windows of Pullman cars and the wide verandas of summer houses. But, of course, he was a veteran tourist.

There are moments when the triviality of the personal note mars the elegiac invocation of the atmosphere. When a Negro porter sets down in the muddy road by the bus the dressing bag which James will be obliged, in the crowded vehicle, to rest upon his knees, the incident gives rise to a long reflection on the general ineptitude of the black man as servant, ending with the sad inquiry if it was for *this* that the old cotton gentry had "fought and fallen"? And when, in New England, echoing the laugh of some Lenox hostess, he mocks the uppishness of the local rustics who expect the summer residents to recognize a cleaning woman under the soubriquet of "washerlady," he seems to be subjecting America to a disdainful monocle. But there are other times when he uses the personal grudge or inconvenience as a source of illumination of the entire horizon. Thus, at the end of the book when he arrives at the Breakers in Palm Beach, the ultima Thule of the American boardinghouse ideal, and finds at ten o'clock in the evening, after a weary day on a train without a proper dining car, that he cannot order a bite to eat, he uses the episode as a brilliant demonstration of the essential rigor, the cruel uniformity, the lack of any real taste which underlies the gaudy, glittering, heartless American world of hotels.

I do not think it is going too far to suggest that in *The American Scene* James was trying his hand at what was — at least for him — a new writing method, a sort of literary impressionism. The book at times becomes almost a novel — at least a novel in the sense used today by Nathalie Sarraute. In New England he turns to romantic speculation to give some kind of life to the bleak villages:

> But the strangest link in the chain, and quite the horridest, was this other, of high value to the restless analyst — that, as the "interesting" puts in its note but where it can and where it will, so the village street and the lonely farm and the hillside cabin became positively richer objects under the smutch of imputation; twitched with a grim effect the thinness of their mantle, shook out of its folds such crudity and levity as they might, and borrowed, for dignity, a shade of the darkness of Cenci-drama, of monstrous legend, of old Greek tragedy, and thus helped themselves out for the story-seeker more patient almost of anything than of flatness.

What the natives will not tell him, the monuments and buildings will. On his first day in America the spandy new summer cottages on the New Jersey shoreline cry out how much they have cost, and in New York Trinity Church bewails the wretched figure which it cuts, dwarfed by the terrible buildings erected to the north — erected, too, by its own board of directors. Such appeals to the author, by edifices and streets, by streams and statues, are usually muted, pathetic. The conclusion is irresistible that James conceived the soul of America as having left her people to lodge in them.

He was not afraid to face unpopular facts. He pointed out that the masses pouring into America from the slums of Europe could never be truly assimilated and that the price of continued immigration would be the loss of the national character and speech as his generation had known it. He saw, too, that the "Americanization" of Europeans, particularly Italians, tended to strip them of their native charm. And he was under no illusion about the racial hatred which smoldered under the dull calm of the southern states. If the handsome and engaging young man who guided him through the Civil War Museum in Richmond was "incapable of hurting a Northern fly," he was still not to be trusted with a southern Negro.

But his deepest divination was of the close connection between American democracy and materialism. He saw that even the snobbishness of the country club was basic-ally superficial, that this curious institution represented the "people," freed from the shackles of European feudalism, enjoying themselves. Such was the true secret of America. The masses *liked* the crowding, the hubbub, the noise, the rush, the money, the glitter. America rep-resented what they had always dreamed of, and they were not disappointed. James, emotionally identifying him-self with the aristocracy of the past with all its traditions and disciplines, felt bewildered and left out. But he never apologized for not liking America. He did not trust it, and he had no faith in its future.

The incident that most summed it all up for him was, as already mentioned, finding no supper at the Breakers. He freely conceded that the majority, for whom such hotels were constructed, were perfectly satisfied with

their temples. They never arrived supperless at ten
o'clock, or if they did they went uncomplaining to bed. But
he wondered, a bit bleakly, where this left the old expatriate:

The fact that the individual, with his preferences, differences,
habits, accidents, might still fare imperfectly even where the
crowd could be noted as rejoicing before the Lord more in-
genuously than on any other human scene, added but another
touch to one's impression, already so strong, of the success with
which, throughout the land, even in conditions which might
appear likely, on certain sides, to beget reserves about it, the
all-gregarious and generalized life suffices to every need.

If James came back to America today, I believe that he
would find it very much as he had anticipated. The buildings are bigger, the pace of life faster, the speech more
debased, the countryside more devastated. But he would
have at least one surprise: the masses are less contented
with their affluence. To recapture the naiveté and enthusiasm of the America of 1904 he would have to go back
to Europe. There he would see that the virus of the twen-
tieth century was not really American at all. It had only
started there. Today, throughout the world, he would find
populations happily engaged in transforming their heritage into highways and supermarkets. But if the master
should cry out in dismay to see the picturesque old squares
of Europe turned into car parks, he might remind himself
that he had been a pioneer. Had he not in 1907 accom-
panied Edith Wharton in her "Motorflight through
France"?

I find after a lifetime of involvement with the works of
James that I am still irreconcilably ambivalent in my attitude to the author of *The American Scene*. For all my con-
tinuing fascination with its amber style, for all my respect

for the integrity of his devotion to his art, I am still irritated when he finds the United States benighted in lacking those two great English institutions: "the parson and the squire." Is this anything but sentimentality for the eighteenth- and nineteenth-century British novel of manners? I suspect that Ezra Pound was shrewdly correct when he implied that James's love of the past was a shallow thing, with little historical consciousness of Rome, Greece, Byzantium, or even the Middle Ages. Put down in the seventeenth century James would have been stripped of ninety percent of his cultivation.

But one had better accept being aggravated by certain aspects of Henry James. Many critics get into trouble when they turn their backs on the problem and put him on a pedestal as an unflawed genius. Behind the great writer who in cathedral tones denounced the materialism and wastefulness of his native land there always lurked the fretful expatriate who scolded the beaches of Florida for their lack of history.

The Memoirs

A Small Boy and Others is the ultimate experience for the Jamesphile — that is, the Jamesphile who has gone a bit over the edge. If one has reached the dangerous point where the parts seem greater than the whole, the individual glimpses grander than the total picture, where the style means more than the "message," then one can ask for nothing richer than the experience of rolling and tumbling with James down the long stream of his personal reminiscence. It is a dazzling exercise of his virtuosity, this evocation of the simple, quaint Albany of his childhood, the arrays of pale, sweet, soon-to-die cousins, the bewildering assortment of quixotic schools in Manhattan, the smells and noises of Broadway, the rich dark air of a sooty, Dickensian London. A valid argument might be made that this is the finest of James's works for the very reason that the artificialities of fiction are absent, that one need not be concerned here with the exaggerated tensions of characters, that loose ends do not have to be tied up or questions answered. It is life itself — the picture needs no justification.

It is also the case that, being of necessity subjective, James has eliminated the old bone of contention which his restricted social view always tossed into the fray between him and his public. The memoir is purely and simply the story of a small boy, a small James, who dedicated himself early and passionately to the role of an observer of life. We have to accept it because it is the *donnée*. One need not fret about whether or not the chosen role was too accepting, too passive. Here is the copious account of just how it all started, the wondrous study of a great observer learning to observe. Is it not an aesthetic experience as fine and keen as that of reading the later novels?

But is it really a different one? *A Small Boy* is a kind of novel because James is trying to give the effect of the past, the *impression* of the past. He did not hesitate, for example, to touch up the family letters from which he quoted. He was intent on reproducing a picture in his mind, and if that picture failed to develop into a precise photograph of the "real" past, he didn't care. To me the most delightful parts of *A Small Boy* are the stories he tells of his relatives and friends. One is perfectly aware, when James turns over the memory of some obscure, long-dead uncle, or of some young warrior, unknown then perhaps to anyone living, falling in a gallant charge before Richmond, that he is allowing his imagination, quite consciously, to play, to speculate, to embroider, to add a little color here and there, to "dramatize," as he always put it, some poor faded fact of the long-lost past. But he doesn't have to do much, and then he can leave his cousins and his friends, pale, beautiful flowers in the tapestry which his fancy has woven out of that past, true or not true to life — who cares? — truer perhaps by the very embellishment of his fancy.

A Small Boy was published in 1913, the same year that

saw the advent of *Swann's Way*. Edith Wharton speaks in her memoirs, *A Backward Glance*, of sending a copy of Proust's novel to James and asserts that he "devoured it in a passion of curiosity and admiration." She even concludes that Proust gave James his last, and one of his strongest, artistic emotions. But Leon Edel doubts that James even read the volume which Mrs. Wharton sent to him. The hideous, preoccupying war broke out — the channel was between the two old friends — Edith Wharton wrote her memoirs twenty years later. I incline to agree with Edel because it is difficult for me to believe that if the author of *A Small Boy* had in fact read *Swann's Way* we should not have found some other evidence of his enthusiasm in his letters and conversations. But except for the Wharton comment the record is bare. She, with hindsight, may have been thinking of what James's attitude *would* have been. For surely he would have been vitally struck by the fact that Proust, like himself, was re-creating — and at the same time in a way creating — a childhood that was to be the product as much of vision as of memory.

James had been initially induced to write his memoirs as a record of his brother William's life. At least it was William's death in 1910 which had tolled the bell of ancient memories and sent his mind back to explore the times and places of his childhood. In *A Small Boy* William's strong and, at least to a younger brother, overpowering personality is still somewhat muted in the amorphous noises of early boyhood, and the volume is dedicated to a general evocation of that early scene. As such it is a triumph. Only in the chapters on the stage does one's interest at all flag. But when James came to the second volume, *Notes of a Son and Brother*, he felt that it behooved him to give a more detailed account of William the young man and artist, and of William the medical student and incipient philosopher, and he emptied whole packets of old letters into the text. It is not that these letters and the personality of William lack interest, but the book becomes more of a family memoir than a work of art.

It still contains, however, some of James's most wonderful chapters. I know of no more moving tribute to a parent than the one devoted to his father. Henry James, Sr., was in many ways the direct opposite of his second son. He believed passionately in living, not in the ordinary sense of a man's active participation in human events, but in the finer meaning of his keeping himself constantly attuned to a greater reality. The "Swedenborgian" stood aside, not like the novelist to be able better to observe his fellowmen, but rather to be in a position to live more intensely. Henry James, Sr., even went so far as to deplore any total dedication to the practice of the arts as a cutting down of life to a single segment of its total circle. The beauty that his son found in the concept of a novel was only a part of the larger beauty that took in heaven and earth. The older James might have been discounted by the younger as a hopeless visionary had it not been for the fact that the father's heart was always big and his mind sound — and perhaps, too, that he never lost his sense of humor. In a word, he was a man, a great man, yet a man, at the same time, who, because of his indifference to the greater public and to any conventional idea of "success," could only be loved by the small circle of his intimates.

Henry saw his father through the eyes of a novelist as well as of a son. He felt the great heart, but he also comprehended the "case." He had, I think, some of the disdain of the consummate artist for the man who fumbles with imponderables, who is always biting off more than he can possibly chew, but I seem to make out that he was also aware of the danger of such disdain and the inferiority of his own heart and love to the paternal heart and love. Henry, assessing his parent, in the end used the best things in himself — his talent as a writer of fiction, his filial respect and affection — along with perhaps a bit of reluctant admiration for a man who was so above the vulgarity of worldly goals that he cared only for the experience of receiving God, or whatever there might be of soul in the universe, through the senses with which he found himself endowed.

The part of *Notes* which makes for the most dramatic contrast with the tribute to Henry James, Sr., is that where the author tells of his own early development as a writer. Here we see him, again and again, strike the note of the passionate observer of life, as opposed to his father's role, with a near frenzy of dedication: "The question of how people looked, and of how their look counted for a thousand relations, had risen before me too early and kept me company too long for me not to have made a fight over it. . . . on the day, in short, when one should cease to live in large measure by one's eyes (with the imagination of course all the while waiting on this) one would have taken the longest step towards not living at all."

If the memoirs contain the richest vein of prose for the dedicated Jamesphile, they also contain passages on which those of the opposite persuasion love to pounce. There are undeniably many sentences where clarity, almost intelligibility, is sacrificed without any corresponding gain in beauty of wording, at times with the positive loss of it. Take, for example, this passage which purports to illustrate James's mother's reaction to the young Harry's whispered warning that a gentleman caller waiting in the

front hall might be "tipsy": "I was to recall perfectly afterwards the impression I so made on her — in which the
general proposition that the gentlemen of a certain group
or connection might on occasion be best described by the
term I had used sought to destroy the particular presump-
tion that our visitor wouldn't, by his ordinary measure,
show himself for one of those."

What a way to say that Mary James was afraid that her
little boy's supposition might be the right one! If there is
anything of beauty or limpidity or even of subtlety added
by the quoted sentence, I have yet to discover it. And I am
almost offended by this way of referring to the death of
Edgar Allan Poe: "The extremity of personal absence had
just overtaken him." Unfortunately, as the work approaches the end, the obfuscations tend to predominate. I
suspect that James was tired and depressed when he was
writing the concluding part of *Notes* and all of *The Middle
Years*. The latter, of course, interrupted by the war, was
never finished. The author reaches finally the point where
he cannot bring up a single memory without telling his
reader that a hundred more breathe upon him, "each with
its own dim little plea." He is so bristlingly aware, as he
casts his eye back on London in 1870, of "intensities of
suggestion," of "numberless reverberations," of "perversities, idiosyncrasies, incalculabilities," that he can never
really get to his subject. He is too anxious to remind one
that anything that does come through will be such a pitiful
part of the pressing horde. It may be unfair to criticize an
unfinished book, but one can still point out that in *A Small
Boy* New York comes through brilliantly without half the
build-up or half the apologies used in the evocation of a
later London.

Out of all the memoirist's hesitations and qualifications

in *Notes* and *The Middle Years*, however, there emerge three fascinating portraits of great writers: Dickens, George Eliot, and Tennyson. So richly had each of these celebrities operated on James's youthful imagination before he met them that he seems almost to begrudge the limiting factor of the personal experience, almost to prefer the unfettered power of fantasy. In Dickens the personal experience was close to nil, consisting only of "an arrest in a doorway" at the Charles Eliot Nortons' in Cambridge during one of the great man's reading tours. The author of *David Copperfield* did not so much as shake the hand of the future author of *The Ambassadors*, but an exchanged glance allowed the latter to rhapsodize over the thrill of taking in, from the former's anguished but disciplined eye, all the pain and horror of his having to husband his declining energies for the "monstrous 'readings'" to which he had so fatally committed himself. The passage is a moving one, but I suspect that there is a good deal of hindsight behind it. Had Dickens not died shortly afterwards, I wonder if James would have remembered him as so desperately conserving his vital forces.

The two glimpses of George Eliot are more authentic, particularly the second. James was taken to call on her and her elderly, respectable lover, George Henry Lewes, by one Mrs. Greville, an indefatigable lion hunter. We are given an unforgettable glimpse of the great novelist, plain and osseous and almost too rapt in a finer air to merit the simple adjective "bored," sitting out the visit of her importunate guests whose departure she will not delay by even a hint of tea, "a conceivable feature of the hour but which was not provided for." And when Lewes hurries to Mrs. Greville's departing carriage to toss back the volumes of her unwelcome gift of poor James's "last," we delight in

the triumph of his delight in having so personal a relation
to the "python" over the more banal one of humiliation. It
is a privilege, after all, to visit the great with an amiable
clown. Mrs. Greville provides the perfect comic reference
for the sketches. How could we see Tennyson better than
in learning that, when she spouted his own verse at the
venerable bard, he responded in "heavily-shovelled coin of
the same mint"? When one thinks of all the writers whom
James was subsequently to meet and know well, Turgenev,
Flaubert, Zola, Daudet, Maupassant, the Goncourts,
Stevenson, Conrad — the list continues until it becomes a
who's who of nineteenth-century literature — one has
some sense of what the interruption of *The Middle Years*
has cost.

The Critic

James has not been generally accorded a very high rating as a literary critic. Certainly, the long essays which he wrote in the last decade of his life are verbose and discursive. I am afraid that "dull" is the only word that will fit "The Lesson of Balzac" where he praises his subject interminably and unilluminatingly, loading him with encomiums that would apply with like propriety to half a dozen other literary masters. There are always delightful *aperçus* in these later essays, as when he describes Rostand as having cut a complete suit out of a corner of the great mantle of Hugo, but they are lost in deserts of verbiage.

As a young man, before his name was known, James showed some of the natural impulse to go for the jugular vein of older writers that is characteristic of young critics of all eras. Thus, we see him at the age of twenty-one telling the readers of the *Nation* not only that *Our Mutual Friend* is the poorest of Dickens's works but that it is poor "with a poverty not of momentary embarrassment, but of permanent exhaustion." And in the same year he found it a "melancholy task" to have to read Walt Whitman's *Drum-Taps* and warned the poet sternly that in order to "sing aright our battles and our glories" it was not enough to be "rude, lugubrious and grim." But as a mature critic he rarely missed the first-rate among contemporary American, English, or French writers, even when their subject material was distasteful to him.

His taste was remarkably sure. He liked Howells; he preferred Sarah Orne Jewett. He liked Zola; he preferred Flaubert. He liked H. G. Wells and Arnold Bennett; he preferred Conrad and R. L. Stevenson. And what was most unusual about his taste was that, unlike most great writers, he had no violent enthusiasms for sycophantic third-raters or disciples who emulated him. Friendship made no matter in this respect; he disliked the novels of Marion Crawford and of Paul Bourget and made few bones about it. Constance Fenimore Woolson was the only inferior writer whom he ever touted for personal reasons, and Leon Edel has written at length on the heavily charged emotional situation that brought this awkwardness about.

It has been said that James in the end liked no novels but his own. This is just not true. He liked his own best, to be sure, but he also liked the works of four such very different authors as Trollope, Maupassant, Flaubert, and Zola. Let us see how he appraised each of these in a retrospective review.

Initially he had had no great opinion of Trollope. Of an Atlantic crossing in 1876 he wrote to his family: "We had also Anthony Trollope who wrote novels in his stateroom (he does it literally every morning in his life, no matter where he may be) and played cards with Mrs. Bronson all

a memory of Henry James and
Joseph Conrad conversing at an afternoon party —
circa 1904.

max
1926

"A memory of Henry James and Joseph Conrad conversing
at an afternoon party — circa 1904" (Beerbohm, 1926)

the evening. He has a gross and repulsive face and manner, but appears *bon enfant* when you talk with him." But
when Trollope died six years later, James wrote a very
moving essay of appreciation. While admitting that Trollope had no system, doctrine, or form, James lauded him
for his knowledge of people:

Trollope's great apprehension of the real, which was what made
him so interesting, came to him through his desire to satisfy us
on this point — to tell us what certain people were and what they
did in consequence of being so. That is the purpose of each of
his tales; and if these things produce an illusion it comes from
the gradual abundance of his testimony as to the temper, the
tone, the passions, the habits, the moral nature, of a certain
number of contemporary Britons.

Trollope was to go on to other fields of English life, but
he never did better than with the clergy. As James put it:

What he had picked up, to begin with, was a comprehensive,
various impression of the clergy of the Church of England and
the manners and feelings that prevail in cathedral towns. This,
for a while, was his specialty, and, as always happens in such
cases, the public was disposed to prescribe to him that path. He
knew about bishops, archdeacons, prebendaries, precentors,
and about their wives and daughters; he knew what these dig-
nitaries say to each other when they are collected together, aloof
from secular ears. He even knew what sort of talk goes on between a bishop and a bishop's lady when the august couple are
enshrouded in the privacy of the episcopal bedroom. This knowledge, somehow, was rare and precious. No one, as yet, had been
bold enough to snatch the illuminating torch from the very
summit of the altar.

James admired Guy de Maupassant as a writer of short
stories, but he made short shrift of him as an analyst of
fiction. In his essay on Maupassant he reduces to nothing
the French writer's theory, naively set forth in the preface
to *Pierre et Jean*, that psychology should be hidden in a
book as it is hidden in reality under the facts of existence.

James immediately raised the question: "From whom is it hidden?" For one person an act may be a sharp, isolated thing: for another it may be hung about with relations and conditions as necessary for recognition as the clothes of one's friends in the street. James goes on to point out that for all Maupassant's deprecation of reference to motives (i.e., psychology), there is one to which he perpetually refers:

If the sexual impulse be not a moral antecedent, it is none the less the wire that moves almost all M. de Maupassant's puppets, and as he has not hidden it, I cannot see that he has eliminated analysis or made a sacrifice to discretion. His pages are studded with that particular analysis; he is constantly peeping behind the curtain, telling us what he discovers there. The truth is that the admirable system of simplification which makes his tales so rapid and so concise . . . strikes us as not in the least a conscious intellectual effort, a selective, comparative process. He tells us all he knows, all he suspects, and if these things take no account of the moral nature of man, it is because he has no windows looking in that direction, and not because artistic scruples have compelled him to close it up.

The piece on Flaubert, written in 1902, seems to me to cut into the very heart of that writer. James has been much criticized for his complaint that Emma Bovary, in spite of the nature of her consciousness and in spite of her reflecting so much that of her creator, is really too small an affair. When I first read this I found it a black mark against James. But in the course of years of rereading *Madame Bovary*, I find myself agreeing with James that if Flaubert could imagine nothing better for his purpose than such a heroine and such a hero, both such limited reflectors and registers, it was by a defect of his mind. And I think that James's distinction between the exotic novels and the bourgeois novels is exact. Flaubert could treat only the themes of the small world of the French middle class, which he despised, unless he took refuge in a distant and romantic past:

He was obliged to treat these themes, which he hated, because his experience left him no alternative; his only alternative was given by history, geography, philosophy, fancy, the world of erudition and of imagination, the world especially of this last. In the bourgeois sphere his ideal of expression laboured under protest; in the other, the imagined, the projected, his need for facts, for matter, and his pursuit of them, sat no less heavily. But as his style all the while required a certain exercise of pride he was on the whole more at home in the exotic than in the famil- iar; he escaped above all in the former connection the associa- tions, the disparities he detested. He could be frankly noble in *Salammbô* and *Saint-Antoine*, whereas in *Bovary* and *L'Education* he could be but circuitously and insidiously so.

James is not here, I take it, saying that *Salammbô* is a better novel than *Madame Bovary*, but that Flaubert is more at his ease in Carthage than Yonville. It was amazing to the American novelist that there were such vast areas of life that Flaubert failed even to suspect as fields of potential exercise for his talent. In James's opinion, the creator of Emma and Charles Bovary never even approached the complications of character in man or woman.

Of all his contemporaries, Zola was the one whom James found most difficult to digest. Seldom have two writers been further apart. When James reviewed *Nana* in 1880, he said that Zola had given his readers "all the bad taste of a disagreeable dish and none of the nourishment." But thirty-four years later, in 1914, when he wrote the retro- spective piece "Émile Zola" for the *Atlantic Monthly*, he had modified his opinion of the French realist writer at least to the extent of admitting that *Les Rougon-Macquart* was a gigantic achievement. His essay is long, and again repeti- tious, but he catches some of the essence of his subject in what he describes as "the wonder of the scale and energy of Zola's assimilations." He makes the point that the strength of Zola lies in his ability to take in and digest immense areas of social facts, but that he inevitably sacrifices to the demonstration and arrangement of these all individual characters of any subtlety, taste, or delicacy. Zola is at his best when he is dealing, as he does in his great novels, in *Germinal* and *L'Assommoir* and *La Débâcle*, with huge crowds made up of the simplest and most animalistic human beings. James describes him as "some mighty animal, a beast of corrugated hide and a portentous snout, soaking with joy in the warm ooze of an African riverside." Ultimately, according to James, facts were to annihilate Zola, and the later novels are dreary deserts to prove that in the long run a total lack of taste is a terrible liability for an author.

James's greatest failure as a critic was with the Russian novelists. The gap here between his strict ideas of form and what he took to be their looseness of construction was too great for him to bridge. Mary McCarthy, in our own time, has suggested that Boris Pasternak was able to write as no other European or American novelist could write because he had not been subjected to James's rules. She believes that an emphasis on technicalities is absolutely fatal to the growth of fiction. Certainly, any rules that leave out the Russians need to be reexamined.

James usually spoke of Tolstoy in terms of guarded respect. His attitude was like that of Delacroix, who said to his students as they passed Ingres's Odalisque in the Louvre: "Messieurs, le chapeau dans la main, mais les yeux fixés à terre." Neither Tolstoy nor Dostoevsky was very much to his taste, and he regarded their effect on other writers as little short of disastrous. Turgenev, on the other hand, he loved and admired, both as a friend and a writer, but then Turgenev was a sort of Russian Henry James, an expatriate who cultivated the French novelists and was regarded as a peer by Flaubert himself. His concern, like James's, was with the fine details of craftsmanship; he was, in the latter's phrase, the novelist's novelist, "an artistic influence extraordinarily valuable and ineradicably established." Too many of Turgenev's rivals, James complained, "appear to hold us in comparison by violent means, and introduce us in comparison to vulgar things."

Did he mean to include Tolstoy among these rivals? It seems likely. For observe how he contrasts him with Turgenev:

> The perusal of Tolstoi — a wonderful mass of life — is an immense event, a kind of splendid accident, for each of us; his name represents nevertheless no such eternal spell of method, no such quiet irresistibility of presentation, as shines, close to us and lighting our possible steps, in that of his precursor. Tolstoi is a reflector as vast as a natural lake; a monster harnessed to his great subject — all human life! — as an elephant might be harnessed, for purposes of traction, not to a carriage, but to a coach house. His own case is prodigious, but his example for others dire: disciples not elephantine he can only mislead and betray.

The compliment, if one was intended, fades under the words "monster" and "elephant." Later James became more candid. When Hugh Walpole wrote to ask him if he did not feel that Dostoevsky's "mad jumble, that flings things down in a heap" was nearer truth than the "picking and composing" of Stevenson, James seized the occasion to state his credo in organ tones:

> Form alone *takes*, and holds and preserves, substance — saves it from the welter of helpless verbiage that we swim in as in a sea of tasteless tepid pudding, and that makes one ashamed of an art capable of such degradations. Tolstoi and D[ostoevsky] are fluid puddings, though not tasteless, because the amount of their own minds and souls in solution in the broth gives it savour

and flavour, thanks to the strong, rank quality of their genius and their experience. But there are all sorts of things to be said of them, and in particular that we see how great a vice is their lack of composition, their defiance of economy and architecture, directly they are emulated and imitated; *then*, as subjects of emulation, models, they quite give themselves away.

Leon Edel maintains that the now-famous term "fluid puddings" has been misunderstood and that James meant so to characterize the novels of the two Russian authors only insofar as they are used as models. But I question this. A fluid pudding is a fluid pudding, whether one eats it or paints it. James evidently considered the process of imitation as a peculiarly revealing one, for it is precisely here, in his opinion, that Tolstoy and Dostoevsky "quite give themselves away," i.e., expose their essential fluidity. But surely these imitators, whoever they were, failed because they saw only formlessness where there was form, just as so many Jamesian imitators have seen only form where there was substance. If we are to rate novelists by the efforts of those who copy them, James will fare quite as badly as Tolstoy or Dostoevsky.

A year later James wrote another letter to Walpole in which he dropped the last pretense of admiration for Tolstoy. If his term "fluid puddings" has been misunderstood, surely there is no misunderstanding the following:

I have been reading over Tolstoi's interminable *Peace and War*, and am struck with the fact that I now protest as much as I admire. He doesn't *do* to read over, and that exactly is the answer to those who idiotically proclaim the impunity of such formless shape, such flopping looseness and such a denial of composition, selection and style. He has a mighty fund of life, but the *waste*, and the ugliness and vice of waste, the vice of a not finer *doing*, are sickening. For me he makes "composition" throne, by contrast, in effulgent lustre!

"The Old Pilgrim comes home" (Beerbohm, 1913)

James's whole life was literature. It was far too serious a subject to be simply clever about. When he felt, as with the Russians, that art was in scant supply, he had to protest from the bottom of his soul. But if the work of a writer with whom he had not been in original sympathy continued to interest him over a period of years, as was the case with Trollope and Zola, then he felt that he had to turn back and study it and find out what tools had been used that were not in his own work shed. If he did not like *War and Peace* (called *Peace and War* by James), let us remember that he liked *Germinal* and *Barchester Towers* and *The House of Mirth* and *Lord Jim* — and, possibly, *Swann's Way*.

With the exception of the Russians, I believe that no great writer has ever been more saturated in and more appreciative of the works of his contemporary peers. Not only did he read them exhaustively; he made a point of getting to know them. That he could read French, Italian, and German was a great advantage — had he been able to read Russian, he might have corrected his astigmatism about Tolstoy. As a critic he generally cared only about making a just assessment of each author. He had made his mark as a writer. It was not necessary for him to gain a name as a gadfly or a humorist or a leader of the avant-garde. It did not matter if he was dull, so long as he was fair. It is this judicial, this priestlike quality that gives to his critical work such value as it has and justifies its place on a shelf under his masterpieces.

INDEX

Index

"Abasement of the Northmores,
The," 119
Adams, Henry, heroes in *Democracy*
and *The Bostonians* compared, 76
"Adina," 36
Albany, N.Y.: James lived in as child,
3; in *The Portrait of a Lady*, 62;
evoked in *A Small Boy and Others*,
152
"Altar of the Dead, The," 93, 118:
source in notebooks, 28–29
Ambassadors, The: international theme
in, 10–11; characterization in,
10–11, 31–32, 132, 133–138; symmetry in, 31–32, 138; style of, 55;
attitude toward sex in, 117; and *The
Spoils of Poynton*, 122; and sensibility, 130; theme of virtuous attachment in, 133–138
American, The, 7, 40: Gothic quality of,
43; and international theme, 44–45,
68; characterization in, 44–46;
melodrama in, 45; dramatized,
102; style of, 102
American Scene, The: based on James's
1904 American tour, 36; on Civil
War soldiers, 76; discussed, 147–
151; style of, 147, 148; marred,
147; prophetic quality of, 147, 149
Amerigo, Prince, character, 120: im-
pressionistic description of, 13–14;

evil in, 124–125; analysis of, 128–
129
Anstruther-Thompson, Mrs., anecdote told at dinner of, 26
Archer, Isabel, character, 11, 57, 109:
and Mme. de Mauves, 38; and international theme, 58, 61, 67;
Americanism of, 62, 63–64, 66;
analysis of, 63–67; and Daisy Miller, 67
"At Isella," characterization of narrator in, 39
"Aspern Papers, The": source in
notebooks, 54; and *Washington
Square* compared, 54–55; lyrical
style of, 55
Assommoir, L' (Zola), 166
Atlantic Monthly, "Émile Zola" appeared in, 165
Augier, Émile, 10, 105
Awkward Age, The, 116, 123: debt to
playwriting experiments, 103; attitude toward sex in, 110, 116–117;
characterization in, 110, 112–113;
and *The Egoist*, 112; style of, 112–
113; and *What Maisie Knew* compared, 114

Backward Glance, A (Wharton), on
James and Proust, 154
Balzac, Honoré de, 86: model for

173

30–35, 37–38, 47, 50–51, 55, 71–72,
80, 90, 101–105, 112–113, 118,
119, 123–124, 130–131, 138, 147,
148, 150, 152, 156–157; middle
period of, 8–9, 13, 45–46, 47, 71,
88, 102, 109, 119; and theater,
9–10, 91, 101–107; relation with
muse, 10, 19; later period of,
11–12, 47, 119, 130; and impressionists, 12–13, 92; last years of,
14–15; description of Venice, 14;
became British subject, 14; destroyed private papers, 17, 86; re-
solve to consider only superior subjects, 20; attained fame with publication of "Daisy Miller," 33;
influence of Hawthorne, 33–35;
development as writer, 34, 156;
toured America in *1904*, 36, 139–
140; historical fiction of, 37; description of Rome, 37; historical
sense of, 37, 57, 151; and use of sex
in fiction, 42, 79–81, 108–117; lived
in Paris, 47; lived in Italy, 47; acquaintance with other writers, 47,
58, 158–159; view of British society,
57–58, 73; and Tennyson, 58, 158,
159; and George Eliot, 58, 158–
159; and Maupassant, 58, 159, 161,
163–164; conservatism of, 60; lack
of sympathy with lower classes, 71;
and Dickens, 72, 75, 86, 158, 160–
161; naiveté as social thinker, 73;
and women's suffrage movement,
78–79; membership in National
Academy, 82; and William James,
82, 154–155; and love as threat to
artist, 85–87; and Oscar Wilde, 85,
107; expatriation of, 86; admired
Sargent, 92; sense of dramatic,
102–103; attended plays in Paris,
105; and Ibsen, 105–106; mental
depression of, 114, 117; views on
democracy and materialism, 149;
and Proust, 154; view of Henry
James, Sr., 155–156; on death of
Poe, 157; and Trollope, 161, 163,
169–170; and Russian novelists,
166–170. *See also individual works*
James, Mary (mother of novelist), 157
James, William, 6, 48: refused mem-

bership in National Academy, 82;
denigrated brother's work, 82; died
1910, 154; inspired brother's
memoirs, 154–155
Jewett, Sarah Orne, James's critical
opinion of, 161
"Jolly Corner, The," 99–100, 142–
143, 146
"Julia Bride," 140, 142

Kemble, Fanny, and plot of
Washington Square, 48, 54

"Lady Barbarina," 68–69
La Farge, John, 35
Lamar, Lucius G. C., model for Basil
Ransom, 76
Lamb House (Rye), 14, 87, 140
Lear, King (character), 28, 73
Lesbianism, of Olive Chancellor, 42,
80, 81
"Lesson of Balzac, The," 160
"Lesson of the Master, The," 84, 87
"Liar, The," source in notebooks, 25
London: impression on young James,
3; James settled in, 6, 48; James din-
ing out in, 6; use of in *The Princess
Casamassima*, 6, 8, 71; failure of *Guy
Domville* in, 10; James's acquain-
tance with other writers in, 58; use
of in *The Portrait of a Lady*, 63;
James's social life in, 84; sexual
freedom in society of, 110; Edwar-
dian and mid-Victorian London
contrasted, 139; evoked in *A Small
Boy and Others*, 152; described in
The Middle Years, 157
"London Life, A," attitude toward sex
in, 109, 117
"Lord Beaupré": source in notebooks,
23–24; characterization in, 23–24
Lord Jim (Conrad), James's opinion of,
170
Louvre, 4, 166
Luxembourg (Paris), 4

McCarthy, Mary, on Boris Pasternak,
166
Madama Butterfly, 44
Madame Bovary (Flaubert), James's
opinion of, 164–165

DATE DUE

WITHDRAWN

PRINTED IN U.S.A.